THE ENDLESS FAIRWAY

The Golfer's Guide To
FLORIDA AND THE CARIBBEAN

EDWARD CHERRY & THE EDITORS OF SOUTHERN LINKS, THE "WHERE TO PLAY" GOLF MAGAZINE

A FIRESIDE BOOK • Published by Simon & Schuster
New York London Toronto Sydney Tokyo Singapore

FIRESIDE
Simon & Schuster Building
Rockefeller Center
1230 Avenue of the Americas
New York, New York 10020

Principal Photographer - Mike Klemme/Golfoto
Supervising Editors - Brett Borton, Mark Brown,
James Max Lane
Designed by Edward Cherry
Manufactured in the United States of America

10 9 8 7 6 5 4 3 2 1

Library of Congress Cataloging in Publication Data
is available.

ISBN: 0-671-74336-8

Contents

Acknowledgments

The author wishes to thank the featured resorts and golf courses, their respective public relations and marketing departments, and the agencies and account executives with which they work for making the successful completion of this book possible; also Mike Klemme and the other contributing photographers for their outstanding art, which made attaching the words relatively easy; Jack Purcell, Max Lane, Cindy Spaulding, Chris Duthie, Brett Borton, Mark Brown, Tracey Coffey, Nicole Fisher, Robyn Wood, Kitty Bartell, Jeannie Hagood and Fred Warren, my colleagues and friends at *Southern Links/Western Links*; Gary Webb, Richard Ross, Lisa Cunard, Carolyn Flamer and Jim Gantt at T-Square Graphics; Jeff Neuman at Simon & Schuster for his patience and prodding; and finally, my lovely wife, Maryanne, who had the great sense of humor necessary for me to get the job done, and who was the perfect traveling companion during these past two years.

Introduction

FOR YEARS I'VE HELD THE widely unpopular opinion that the traditional beliefs about the game of golf being "invented" along the windswept shores of Scotland some 500 years ago were primarily the result of good public relations. Think about it. Isn't it a bit ludicrous to think that during the previous millenia no one else tending his flock—or herd, or gaggle—didn't aim a stone at a point on the horizon and send it forth off the end of a stick? (No doubt the first such "shot" struck in this manner was a full-banana slice.)

> **"This earliest version of 'the game' involved neither slope ratings nor slow play warnings from course marshals nor discounted rates after 3 p.m."**

This earliest version of "the game" was played solely for the fun of it (and to relieve the boredom inherent in such endeavors), and involved neither slope ratings nor slow play warnings from course marshals nor discounted rates after 3 p.m.

If I remember my high school history correctly, the Scots of the 15th century were a particularly self-destructive lot. Leave it to a people with such an immolative bent to begin keeping score, which begat the writing of rules, which begat the need for a handicap system, which, of course, begat the occasional fist fight behind the clubhouse after the annual member/guest tournament.

As I said, this opinion is rather unique and has caused a few problems with my colleagues at *Southern Links*, most notably traditionalists such as editor-in-chief Mark Brown, and hall of fame golf writer Dick Taylor (who, I think, secretly believes that golf *really* was invented somewhere around Pinehurst, N.C., shortly after he moved there), and CBS golf commentator Ben Wright, who would gladly have me pressed into lifetime service in the British Navy as a galley slave—if he couldn't first convince the proper authorities to have me pilloried in the town square so the golfing public could, at their leisure, bean me with feathery balls (not balata) or take a whack at me with a hickory shaft (not boron-graphite).

Be that as it may, whether the game of golf was in fact devised by the Seminole Indians of Florida, or the Arawak Indians of the Bahamas or the Carib Indians of the West Indies, or even by the Scots themselves, it obviously was intended to be played where the climate is conducive, the surroundings picture perfect, the golf championship caliber, the accommodations first class and the service impeccable. That, my golfing friends, means Florida and the Caribbean.

First a word on my golf credentials: Ordinary. I carry a 12 handicap that floats to a 14 during mid winter and mid summer, the times when I play the least. That number means only that some days (rarely) I break 80; some days (frequently) it barely gets me into the clubhouse under three digits. But if there is in fact a golf "bug," it bit me around 1980, hard, and I've never, thankfully, fully recovered. I love the game as I doubt I could ever love another. My clubs are never more than 50 yards from me (just in case), I fix at least three ball marks per green, replace the divot (when I'm lucky enough to

The author identified the photo below as either the Southeastern coast of Scotland or Mullet Bay Beach on the Dutch side of St. Maarten.

Night falls on the Boca Raton Resort & Club on the Intracoastal Waterway in Boca Raton, Fla.

take one) or fill it with sand, and always wave faster-playing golfers "through," although if they play faster than I do it's something more akin to polo than it is to golf.

I analyze the swing of every tour pro on television, knowing full well it is has nothing whatsoever to do with the way I play, and I've purchased every new club, ball, accoutrement and device that's come on the market in the so-far fruitless search for the one magical ingredient that's been missing from my game. I'm thinking that my credentials are probably a lot like yours.

My Florida experience comes from the eleven years I lived in the Miami area—looking back, years that could have been better spent, golfwise—and the nearly five years of travel as an editor at *Southern Links* and *Western Links* magazines. During those five years I've signed on to every press trip that's headed south from our offices on Hilton Head Island, and not surprisingly the majority of those trips were to the Sunshine State—whose 1,000-plus (and climbing) courses could take years (hopefully) of careful research and reporting.

But "vacationing" in the Caribbean began even earlier for me than Florida, or golf. One of my first duty stations as a Marine Corps private was as a Fleet Marine attached to the U.S. Navy in the Caribbean. We spent six months cruising from island to island (the training we *endured* between stopovers is nearly forgotten 25 years later), anchoring in the harbors of some of the most interesting and delightful of the islands—including Grenada, San Juan and St. Thomas—for four or five days of liberty, as it is so appropriately labeled in the armed forces. Imagine if you will a 17-year-old New Jersey delinquent who had never been further west than Philadelphia being transported to a tropical paradise of which he had seen only pictures. At the time I didn't even *know* anyone who'd been there.

The enthusiasm of that 17-year-old remains today, after countless trips to Florida and the Caribbean for both business and pleasure. The line between the two is very, very fine.

The author leaves a ball in the sand while negotiating one of the Caribbean's "natural" hazards—the clothing-optional beach at Jamaica, Jamaica resort in Runaway Bay.

I realize there's a lot of work still to be done. There are many fine resorts left to be visited, many great golf courses left to be played. I hope to make that my life's work. And I hope you enjoy this "reminiscence" of the trip thus far as much as I had taking it.

Northern Florida

THE EDITORS OF THIS PUBLICATION WANTED ME TO FILL THIS space with information about area attractions, climate, transportation options, etc., when traveling to the golf resorts of Northern Florida. I didn't have the heart to tell them they've got the wrong guy for the job. First of all, I live in South Carolina, so transportation to Northern Florida for me is two hours by car, due south. To anyone traveling from further away I offer this advice: Get in your car and drive southeast. If you live in the Midwest or Northeast you can make your trip by automobile a grand golf adventure, perhaps spending a day or two in Pinehurst, N.C., or Myrtle Beach, S.C., or perhaps on Hilton Head Island. You could follow that with a few days in the sea islands of Georgia and just be hitting your stride when you cross the border into Florida. If that's too much time for you to spend at once, obviously you need to call your travel agent and make the appropriate arrangements. He or she will provide all the assistance you require, and a lot more than I could give you here.

The weather in Northern Florida is perfect for golf year-round, never too hot in summer, never too cold in winter. Spring and fall are my

favorite times to travel there, although my wife and I have spent a few winter weekends at Amelia Island—wrapped in sweatshirts while shelling on the beach and wearing gloves on the golf course—and loved it. You've heard of the occasional north-Florida freeze, and between late December and early March there is a chance you'll witness it first-hand. There is always that possibility. But you run the risk of inclement weather every time you leave your home, no more so here than anywhere else.

As far as area attractions are concerned, I must admit I'm not really up to snuff about such things. I've never been one for reserving a space at one of the finest golf resorts in the country, then going elsewhere to find something to do. If you can't find it here, where are you going to go to look for it? (But Daytona Beach, St. Augustine and Jacksonville are three of the places I'd go first, if I were so inclined.)

But if you're looking for reasons to travel to Northern Florida, perhaps for the first time, I now offer two of the best: 1) the photo on the left of the links-like Amelia Island Plantation, with its stunning beaches, superlative accommodations and championship golf and tennis; and 2) the photo above of the Sheraton Palm Coast Resort, with four of the finest golf courses in one place, anywhere. That's the best I can do. It should be enough.

Amelia Island Plantation

The environmental jewel of the Golden Isles

AMELIA ISLAND NEAR JACKSONVILLE, Fla., has been called a lot of things, like "Hilton Head with Florida beaches," and "A great South Florida resort...misplaced." But I think my cousin Vinny from Brooklyn put it best when he said: "Amelia? *Nice.*" Cousin Vinny may be short on words but he's long on good taste (He knows, for example, that the finest cuisine in New York is a slice of thick-crust pizza and a chocolate egg cream to wash it down), so when Vinny talks, people listen....or else.

Cousin Vinny is right, of course. Amelia is nice, very nice. Its 1,250 acres are sited along the southern tip of the 13-1/2-mile island, the southernmost in the famous Golden Isle chain, and its original development was begun by a gentleman of some renown in that particular field of endeavor, Charles Fraser. Fraser was fresh from his overwhelmingly successful Sea Pines Plantation on Hilton Head Island, and when the resort first opened in 1974 it truly seemed that the sky was the limit. Unfortunately—then, as now—the "limit" is set by your local bank officer, and between 1974 and 1978 Amelia was left to meander aimlessly in that great abyss with other similarly unsuccessful ventures that don't die, and don't fade away, either.

But the plan, if not the execution, was a good one, and when Midwest businessman and Amelia Island property owner Richard L. Cooper purchased all of Amelia's assets and undeveloped property in 1978, he added these items to the initial agenda: Turn Amelia into a full-fledged resort, maintain the pristine environment and keep the golf coming.

Pete Dye designed the original 27 holes of Amelia Links—the Oakmarsh, Oysterbay and Oceanside courses—in the early 1970s; friend Fraser brought him to Amelia following their collaboration at Harbour Town Golf Links in Sea Pines. All three courses are distinctively

different in character, but all represent the classic style of "early" Dye designs: simple and natural.

The golf courses of Amelia Links all feature tight fairways and small greens (which before their recent renovation had grown impossibly tiny) that require the utmost precision in your iron play (The longest course in the rotation is Oakmarsh at only 3,263 yards, so snappy iron work is prerequisite). Oysterbay is thought of by many as the most dramatic of the three, with marsh directly in play on four of the nine holes and clearly visible from the others.

Oceanside, however, is the most photographed and the most easily recognized. Its three-hole stretch along the Atlantic Ocean—the 341-yard, par-4 fourth, the 133-yard, par-3 fifth and the 178-yard, par-3 sixth—is widely regarded as the premier tract on the Amelia Links courses; perhaps the best and most beautiful links-style golf in the Eastern U.S.

In 1987 a new course was added, the heralded Long Point course designed by Tom Fazio. The setting for Long Point offered ocean frontage, expansive marshlands, rolling terrain, dense forests of live oak and pine and natural lakes and lagoons. At 6,750 yards from the back tees, Long Point's strength on the shorter, windier front nine is its tight landing areas; on the back its length becomes more of a factor. The 222-yard, par-three 12th hole and the 440-yard, par-four 18th are long enough as is, but

Oceanside's scenic three-hole stretch along the Atlantic includes the par-4, 341-yard fourth and two par-3s, the 133-yard fifth and the 178-yard sixth.

throw in the coastal breezes that are common in this area and both greens are virtually unreachable in regulation.

Guests at Amelia Island Plantation are quartered in 1,100 rooms ranging from three-story buildings with one-, two- and three-bedroom villas to townhomes with private pools to patio-type cluster homes and single-family homes.

The resort also features a large-scale tennis facility called Racquet Park, with 21 courts (four additional courts are spread around the property), and a year-round tournament schedule which has included the prestigious Bausch & Lomb women's tennis championship and continues as the site of the Du Pont All American Tennis Championship.

Dining at Amelia is an experience in itself, with fine cuisine in the Dune Side Club with its international menu and a complementary wine list. The Verandah at Racquet Park is family oriented but no less enjoyable, and the Beach Club Restaurant prides itself on its charcoal-broiled prime beef. Cocktails and entertainment are served up in the Admiral's Lounge in the Amelia Island Inn.

If you're at all familiar with the work of Charles Fraser, either at Sea Pines or Amelia, you know that first and foremost was the charge to leave the land as close to the way you found it as possible. Amelia Island Plantation has continued that tradition of preservation, despite its incredible growth as both a resort and a community. As cousin Vinny might say: "Yo! Got a problem with that?" ■

AMELIA ISLAND PLANTATION— AMELIA ISLAND, FLA.

LOCATION: Hwy. A1A South, Amelia Island, FL 32034; 30 minutes from Jacksonville International Airport.

ACCOMMODATIONS: One-, two-, three-, and four-bedroom villas and pool villas and cluster homes; the Amelia Island Inn.

DINING/ENTERTAINMENT: Six restaurants including the Dune Side Club, international menu; The Verandah at Racquet Park; and the Beach Club Restaurant; two lounges including the Admiral's Lounge in the Amelia Island Inn; property-wide room service.

AMENITIES: 45 holes of golf; 25 tennis courts; health and fitness center including heated indoor lap pool; sailing; horseback riding; bicycling; paddleboats; youth program.

RATES: Accomodations begin at $128 for villas; Inn rooms from $175.

RESERVATIONS: Call (800) 456-2000.

Marriott's Bay Point Resort

YOU WONDER WHAT BRUCE DEVLIN and Robert von Hagge were thinking when they designed the Lagoon Legend course at Marriott's Bay Point Resort in Panama City Beach. Did they know then that it would become the home of the PGA Tour Qualifying School? Or that it would host the USGA Junior Tour event televised on ESPN? Or that the course logo would be a fire-breathing dragon? (Which is appropriate considering the *burn* that Lagoon Legend's 7,000 yards of water-encased fairways, deep and abundant bunkering and "eccentric" pin placements will put on you.)

One gets the feeling Devlin and von Hagge were aware of all of the above when they crafted this devil of a layout—on which triple-digit scores and three-sleeve nines are not at all uncommon—named by *Golf Digest* as "the second most difficult course in America."

You also get the feeling that Marriott knows something about finding sites for their golf resort courses that provide the maximum in aesthetics and challenge.

The 1,100 acres of Bay Point, for example, border the Gulf of Mexico and are nestled amidst a wildlife preserve peninsula and St. Andrews Bay. The Lagoon Legend course was shaped through and around the rolling hillsides and Lowcountry-like marshes, and utilizes the natural and man-made lagoons and the inlets and channels as hazards on 16 of its holes.

The outward nine at Lagoon Legend is longer (well over 3,500 yards) than the inward half, but its wide fairways and ample landing areas are "forgiving" if you're hitting it fairly straight. The first two holes, however, dogleg to the right (as do the first three holes on the back nine), so a hard draw or a dreaded snap hook puts you out of bounds or in the water without much effort. For the most part your driver should remain in the bag, except perhaps on the 450-yard third hole, a straightaway par-four that let's you air it out without cause for concern. Make your number on the front if you can; you probably won't like the one you end up with on the back.

Nos. 10, 11 and 12 are scoreable—a 376-yard, par-four dogleg right, a 193-yard par-three and a 512-yard par-five, respectively. Thirteen begins the lunch-eating portion of this course with a 300-yard par-four that doesn't read like much on the card but which is flanked—surrounded really (and accessible only via a walkway)—with the Tai Tai Swamp. The *eight* I posted here was a pretty good one, actually, considering I air-mailed two into the swamp before I left the tee box.

Nos. 14 and 15 involve water, sand, trees, high grass and bunkers, and at 434 and 454 yards these par-fours require a little extra encouragement to get home in regulation. Getting there and getting down are two different things; the well-manicured, true-rolling and lightning-fast putting surfaces encourage a certain degree of golfing stupidity, such as flying one out of the bunker on the left into the water on the right of 14, and rolling one out of the bunker on the right of 15 across the speedy green into the bunker on the left. (At least I took the water out of play.)

So there I was, headed for the tee of No. 16, a cool eight-over on the back nine, when I struck a low-boring 3-iron into the wind of the 197-yard par-three. The ball took two short bounces and rolled directly toward the hole. Somehow it managed to rim the cup and

Marriot's Bay Point Resort features the "second most difficult course in America," Lagoon Legend.

come to rest about six inches behind the hole; the closest I've ever come to a hole-in-one, at a time when I most needed it. Too bad...but that's golf.

Seventeen is a dogleg right/dogleg left par-five of 519 yards which is easily played in par (3-wood, 5-wood, full wedge)—not very exciting when you're so desperately in need of a birdie. But making par is a good habit to develop, especially when you're heading to the 18th of Lagoon Legend, a 382-yard par-four that plays over water from the tee to an island landing area, then back over the water to the green. Suffice to say my seven-over didn't hold up, but my 87 (41-46) felt a lot better than it looked, which maybe is what Devlin and von Hagge had in mind all along.

The Club Meadows course rounds out the golf facilities, and at 6,913 yards this Willard Byrd design provides all the length and challenge you can handle. Admittedly, I scored eight strokes better on Club Meadows than on Lagoon Legend, so it ranks up there among my *favorite* Florida golf courses (those on which I've broken 80).

The resort also comprises five swimming pools, a 12-court tennis center, yacht club and marina for boats up to 120 feet, fishing, fitness...and finesse in the elegant restaurants and lounges.

There's also a private paddle-wheel river boat for excursions to Shell Island and sunset cocktail cruises. You should know beforehand that the *Island Queen* is equipped with life preservers, and the only thing throwing yourself overboard will get you (assuming you've played Lagoon Legend that day) is wet. ■

MARRIOTT'S BAY POINT RESORT— PANAMA CITY BEACH, FLA.

LOCATION: 100 Delwood Beach Road, Panama City Beach, FL 32411; one-hour flight from Atlanta.

ACCOMMODATIONS: 386 rooms, suites and villas with bay, lake and golf views.

DINING/ENTERTAINMENT: Terrace Court, private yacht club setting featuring nouvelle cuisine and tableside service; Fiddler's Green, fresh seafood in a casual atmosphere; Teddy Tucker's, raw bar and sandwiches; Sunset Grill, beach-style surf and turf; Greenhouse, fine food in a garden setting; Circe's, lounge with nightly entertainment; Sunset Pub.

AMENITIES: 36 holes of golf; 12 tennis courts; health and fitness center; five swimming pools; sailing; croquet; bicycling and jogging on resort's nature trails; youth program.

RATES: From approx. $90 to $150 per night.

RESERVATIONS: Call (904) 234-3307.

Sheraton Palm Coast Resort

HOLE FOR HOLE, BUNKER FOR bunker, hazard for hazard, the Sheraton Palm Coast Resort has as many great golf courses in one location as any northern Florida resort; perhaps *any* Florida resort, period. And if that were all it had to offer it would still be worth the price of admission. But the Sheraton Palm Coast bills itself as northeast Florida's all-new sports resort, and the activities and amenities it offers seem to qualify it for that designation.

The resort doesn't just *offer* these activities, either; it assaults you with them. Mandatory equipment for a stay at Palm Coast is a map of the property and a Daytimer. If you sign on for the full program you'll be up and running at dawn and getting back to your hotel room about the time the street lights come on. You will never, ever run out of things to do here. If you do, call the general manager. He'll find something to keep you occupied.

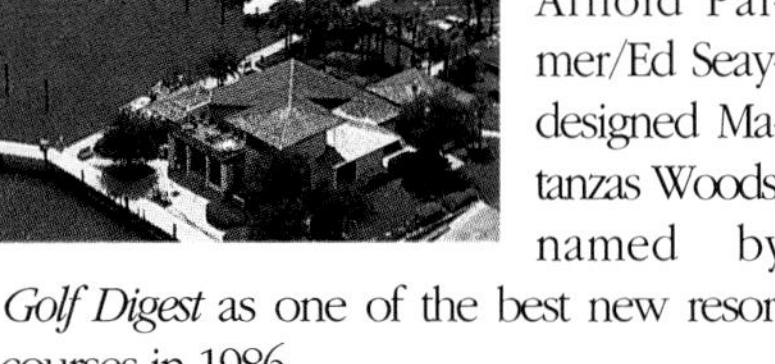

Before we get too carried away here, perhaps we'd better zero in on the main event: the four courses, including the members-only (and guests of the hotel) Hammock Dunes course designed by Tom Fazio. Hammock Dunes opened in 1989 with a Scottish-links design that was the envy of many designers in the industry. The par-72, 6,820-yard masterpiece offers the opportunity to run the ball onto many of the moderately undulating putting surfaces, a luxury not often found these days.

On the Palm Coast property are Pine Lakes, Palm Harbor, and the Arnold Palmer/Ed Seay-designed Matanzas Woods, named by *Golf Digest* as one of the best new resort courses in 1986.

At nearly 7,000 yards, the par-72 Matanzas Woods course is a gut check from the championship tees, as you would expect from a course that has hosted the PGA Tour Qualifying School.

But the greens are "fair" (if there is such a thing is this game), and smart fairway-wood and long-iron play will get you on or near the greens in regulation. From there it's up to you.

Pine Lakes is another Palmer/Seay design, in much the same vein as Matanzas Woods. It too is in the 7,000-yard range, and it too requires long-club prowess. I never hit into a sand bunker at Pine Lakes, but they looked to be a bit deeper and a bit fluffier than either Matanzas or Palm Harbor. (In fact, "Fluffy" is the nickname we gave one of our playing partners when he took three to get out of one.)

Palm Harbor is deceptive at 6,555 yards: You've got to hit shorter clubs, but you've got to hit them hard. There are many tee shots and approaches that seem to trap you in the middle of, say, a 4- or 5-iron (for me about a 12-yard difference), which, considering the well-protected putting surfaces, could be an eight- or nine-stroke difference in your score. Lee Trevino and Nancy Lopez worked it out okay in 1978 when they won the Mixed Team Championship here, so maybe it's just me.

Amenity-wise you need to "pack a lunch" at Palm Coast. There are boats for charter or rental, and no license is required for fishing the Intracoastal or offshore. You can work out at the Harbor Club's recreation island on Universal weight machines, or you can sign up for the daily aerobics classes.

The Palm Coast Player's Club offers 16 courts (10 clay, four hard surface and two grass), eight of which are lighted for night play, and two outdoor racquetball courts. Swimming pools are located at the hotel, Harbor Club and Beach Club, whirlpools can be found on the hotel pool deck and at Harbor Club, and separate men's and women's saunas are available. The free shuttle will have you on the white-sand northern Florida beach (halfway between Daytona and St. Augustine) in a matter of minutes, where you can spend a quiet, uncrowded afternoon sunning or shelling.

In short, every day is a full day at Sheraton Palm Coast Resort. It's nice to know that when you're ready to go home your fun ticket will be completely punched...and that you'll finally be going someplace where you can relax. ■

SHERATON PALM COAST RESORT — PALM COAST, FLA.

LOCATION: 300 Clubhouse Dr., Palm Coast, FL 32137; 80 miles from Jacksonville.

ACCOMMODATIONS: 154 rooms including two VIP suites, all with waterfront views of marina or Intracoastal Waterway.

DINING/ENTERTAINMENT: Flagler's, adjacent to lobby serving breakfast, lunch and dinner; Champions Restaurant (Pine Lakes C.C.), lunch and dinner in club setting; Beach Club, snacks; Henry's Good Spirits.

AMENITIES: Access to four 18-hole golf courses in immediate area; two swimming pools (one heated); fully equipped fitness center with Universal equipment and aerobics; 16 tennis courts (eight lighted).

MEETING FACILITIES: 11,500 square feet of flexible space accommodating groups to 350.

RATES: From $110 to $160 (high season).

RESERVATIONS: Call (800) 325-3535.

Sandestin Beach Resort

SANDESTIN RESORT IN DESTIN, FLA., has been called the "jewel of the Emerald Coast," the name given the area of northwest Florida between Panama City and Pensacola along the Gulf of Mexico. It's appropriate: The waters of the Gulf in this region are a shimmering shade of turquoise that are quite nearly phosphorescent in the early morning and late afternoon sun.

But the resort is also a jewel in the golf department, with two 18-hole, par-72 courses designed by Tom Jackson that will test your skill with tight fairways and well-bunkered greens on the 6,670-yard Links course, or test your patience on the 7,210-yard Baytowne course. There's also the nine-hole Troon course, with several par-fives in the 600-yard range that require a little extra *oomph!* on your first, second and sometimes third shots.

The Sandestin Tennis Center is also jewel-like, with 16 courts in three surfaces: clay, hard and grass. (Yes, grass! Sandestin is one of the few resorts in the country to offer them.) *Tennis* magazine ranks Sandestin among the top 50

tennis resorts in the U.S., and *World Tennis* magazine gives Sandestin five-stars. The Center hosts the annual Professional Grass Court Tournament, which a number of tennis pros on their way to Wimbledon use as a warmup.

Gulf Coast fishing is at its best off the Sandestin beaches (the site of the Destin Fishing Rodeo each October and a dozen or so other tournaments), and the Baytowne Marina or the Destin Yacht Club will arrange charters to search for the mackerel, sailfish, cobia and marlin that run these waters. And you can always drop a line in the stocked lakes that run nearby.

One resort addition that has caused some excitement is the recently opened Sports/Spa & Clinic, a health and fitness complex that comprises a sports science laboratory, full-service spa, health center, medical clinic and corporate wellness programs, which one of the facility's organizers calls "a mall of preventive medicine." Program participants will be tested and analyzed to determine strength, oxygen consumption, abstract reasoning abilities and weakness, then provided a "prescription" for improvement. Minor surgery can be performed in the clinic, and I can't think of a better place to recuperate than lounging by one of the resort's many swimming pools. Nautilus will also showcase its "next generation" equipment here, and has chosen the clinic as its primary national training site.

Sandestin Resort has five main restaurants on property, but the Elephant Walk Restaurant and Lounge is the main attraction. The uniquely styled building was inspired by the movie of the same name and is an Asian oasis serving seafood, fowl and beef in ways I'm sure you've never imagined. Babe's Seafood House offers a Friday night seafood buffet during the season, and Harry T's is a casual eatery/meetery with 1930s memorabilia adorning the walls and over 90 items on the menu.

But it's the Sports/Spa & Clinic that most moves me about Sandestin. Until I went there, my editor had me convinced that "corporate wellness" was taking Sundays off, and that the prescription for improved performance was "Get back to work!" ■

SANDESTIN BEACH RESORT — DESTIN, FLORIDA

LOCATION: 5500 U.S. Highway 98 East, Destin, FL 32541; 45 minutes from Pensacola.

ACCOMMODATIONS: 175 rooms at the Inn at Sandestin; villas and condominiums overlooking Gulf, Bay or golf course.

DINING/ENTERTAINMENT: A variety of restaurants and lounges including the Elephant Walk Restaurant, Continental dining in casual elegance; Harry T's Boathouse, fun and fine food; Babe's Seafood House; The Marina Cafe, cocktail lounge and oyster bar.

AMENITIES: 45 holes of golf; 16 tennis courts; swimming pools; fully equipped fitness center; boating; fishing.

MEETING FACILITIES: 16 rooms offering 17,000 square feet for groups to 1,500.

RATES: Call for rates and golf packages.

RESERVATIONS: (800) 874-3950.

Marriott at Sawgrass Resort

SADLY, I'M A GOLFING WANNA-BE. I wanna-be able to hit a fairway wood 235 yards into a par-five; I wanna-be able to get up-and-down from a greenside bunker 75 percent of the time; I wanna-be a +2 handicap; and I wanna-be standing here telling you that I brought the golf courses at Sawgrass to their knees. That's the sad part—I can't do any of these things.

I'm sure it was related to the anxiety I experienced walking onto the first tee of the first course I played at the resort, the Tournament Players Club at Sawgrass Stadium Course, home of The Players Championship and site of the most photographed hole in all of golf, the 132-yard Island Hole 17th.

And I suppose the anxiety was related to the rankings this course has received from national golf publications, such as No. 54 of the 100 greatest courses in the world according to *Golf* magazine, and No. 32 of America's 100 greatest courses according to *Golf Digest.* I don't know why I pay attention to such things. If it were a book review or movie review I'd ignore it, yet someone says "Tough course!" and I immediately take it to heart.

But it is a tough course, no getting around it. Pete Dye saw to that when he stretched it to 6,857 yards and fashioned water into the layout 18 times. That's right, all 18 holes of this par-72 have water in play; I know that from experience. It was the first (and hopefully the last) time I ever *had to* buy balls at the turn, and I didn't just buy a *sleeve*, if you know what I mean. Why, I left a sleeve on No. 17 alone. I suppose I needed the beating I took that day. I was a little cocky about my game coming in, but it's difficult playing toughguy with your Bermudas down around your ankles.

That should be as bad as it gets. The Valley Course, another Dye design, is a links-style layout that plays 6,838 yards to a par of 71. While not docile, the course is manageable if you can get a 3- or 4-wood 225 yards over water to the green of No. 2, and keep your ball away from the bulkheading on No. 4. Unfortunately, that day I couldn't do either.

The Sawgrass Country Club Course is a 27-hole challenge designed by Ed Seay and ranked in the top 25 of the best resort courses in the U.S. The West/South rotation (7,115 yards) was the one I played, and if your best drive of the day is in the neighborhood of 225 yards, you've got a problem. I did.

The Oak Bridge Golf Club Course (also by Seay) is a meager 6,345 yards, and with a par of 70 I thought I had a chance to make something of a comeback. But the pine, palm and oak trees that line many of the fairways didn't have a lot of *give* in them that day, and I limped home having *not* broken 90 the entire weekend.

Fortunately the surroundings will help you forget the past—even the most recent past—with 2-1/2 miles of pristine beach, lush tropical foliage inside and out, 15 acres of water encircling the hotel and 350 acres of freshwater lakes and lagoons. The hotel's seven-story atrium offers a spectacular view of the 13th hole of the Stadium Course, and the old-fashioned trolley tram is a pleasant diversion and a great way to see the resort's 4,800 acres.

Dining at Sawgrass is elegant in the Augustine Room, with Continental cuisine and a wine list of some repute, or casual in the Cafe on the Green, an all-day, family-style restaurant with buffets, burgers and seafood specialties.

Champs is the hot night spot on the property, featuring nightly live entertainment and cocktails with little umbrellas and the like. I particularly enjoyed Cascades, an intimate, multi-level lounge with piano music and a waterfall in the background.

The Marriott is also the official hotel of the Association of Tennis Professionals (ATP), and features a 10-court tennis complex, professional instruction and a pro shop. And after the weekend I spent on the golf courses, I think I now wanna-be a tennis player. ■

MARRIOTT AT SAWGRASS RESORT

LOCATION: 1000 TPC Boulevard, Ponte Vedra Beach, FL 32082; 20 minutes from Jacksonville International Airport.

ACCOMMODATIONS: 557 guest rooms, suites and villas

DINING/ENTERTAINMENT: Augustine Room, classic and American cuisine in Old World elegance; Cafe on the Green, all-day family dining; 100th Hole, poolside; Champs, cocktails and entertainment; Cascades.

AMENITIES: 99 holes of golf; 10-court (four lighted) tennis complex; 2-1/2-miles of private beach; three swimming pools; health club; fitness center; biking; jogging.

MEETING FACILITIES: 35,000 square feet of space including Masters Ballroom and The Tournament Hall exhibit area (102 booths).

RATES: From approx. $90 to $120 per night.

RESERVATIONS: Call (800) 457-GOLF.

Bluewater Bay

Casual elegance in the heart of the Emerald Coast

THERE'S SOMETHING COMFORTING about scanning a roadmap and finding a town named Niceville. As far as vacation destinations go, it's so much more reassuring than, say, *Dry Gulch* or the dreaded *Mud Flats*. So it's only fitting that one of northwest Florida's finest and most secluded resorts is located in just such a town.

Bluewater Bay is a residential/resort community that prides itself on its 1,800 acres of peaceful, unspoiled surroundings, its lavish resort amenities and its luxurious accommodations, all blended harmoniously inside a virtual perimeter of nature's handiwork. To the south of the resort is a freshwater lake; bordering it to the west are 38 miles of Choctawhatchee Bay; to the north a state park; and to the east a federal preserve. If Grizzly Adams played golf, this is where he would do it.

Despite its somewhat out-of-the-way location, Bluewater Bay offers an amenities package as extensive as the familiar haunts, with a little something extra: bay cruising on the *Sunquest*, 48 feet of sailing excellence adorned with teak and brass and "Old World" charm. *Sunquest* may be chartered for sunset or moonlight cruises, half- or full-day sails, weekend getaways or five-day adventures, with an all-inclusive price that appears exceptionally reasonable.

Naturally, sailing is secondary to golf, which is provided by three nine-hole courses—Bay, Lake and Marsh—that feature a minimum of water hazards, a moderate amount of bunkering and just about all the length you can handle. The nines run from 2,615 yards to a healthy 3,485, and the layouts are, well, nice. And you don't have to drive through *Death Valley* to get there. ■

Bluewater Bay
P.O. Box 247
Niceville, FL 32588

LOCATION: 15 minutes from Ft. Walton Beach/Eglin Airport; daily flights from Atlanta.

ACCOMMODATIONS: Variety of apartments, villas, townhomes and free-standing homes with bay or golf views.

DINING/ENTERTAINMENT: Flags, elegant dining at affordable prices for dinner only, pasta, seafood and steaks; Greenhouse Bar & Grill, sandwiches and chef's specials.

AMENITIES: 18 holes of golf (Tom Fazio/Jerry Pate); day and night tennis; 120-slip full-service marina, rental boats, fishing charters, windsurfing; three swimming pools; private beach.

RATES: Call for rates.

RESERVATIONS: Call (800) 874-2128.

Killearn Country Club & Inn

IF YOU'VE SEEN THE TELEVISION commercials where the proprietor of the bed-and-breakfast runs around in a frenzy because the alarm didn't go off and now she'll have to serve her guests instant coffee instead of fresh brewed, you know what Killearn Country Club & Inn in northern Tallahassee is like. Not the coffee, and not the proprietor in a frenzy, but the quaint, charming atmosphere of a true country inn, and the personalized service that comes with it.

Killearn's conference facilities are small (tiny, really) by comparison to the coastal resorts, but their clientele usually travels in smaller groups, such as top-level executives in for high-level board meetings and a few holes of golf afterward, and before, and during.

Golfers consider their vacations pretty high-level stuff, too, so naturally Killearn is the perfect setting for families, golf groups of four to 40, and couples who need to take time out to enjoy the privacy and serenity of the surroundings.

The golf is good here, good enough to annually host the LPGA's Centel Classic, good enough to test the mettle of any low-handicapper and good enough to make the golfing experience enjoyable for the beginner. The three nines—North, South and East—run from 2,700 yards from the red tees of the North to a whopping 3,532 yards from the blue tees of the South.

The rolling fairways and moss-draped live oaks at Killearn add a certain Georgia flavor to the courses, and the full-swing design (27 holes of it) will put you to sleep at night as soon as your head hits the pillow. Hmm....Better make mine decaf. ■

Killearn Country Club & Inn
100 Tyron Circle
Tallahassee, FL 32308

LOCATION: 20 minutes from Tallahassee National Airport.

ACCOMMODATIONS: 39 rooms including 20 (standard) inn rooms and 19 in the lodge.

DINING/ENTERTAINMENT: Oakview Dining Room, fine dining, steaks, seafood (Tues. - Sat.); 19th Hole Mixed Bar & Grill, casual, appetizers, steaks, pasta and sandwiches, open seven days.

AMENITIES: Three nine-hole golf courses, practice facility; eight tennis courts (four lighted for night play); swimming pool, kiddie pool; Hydra-Gym exercise facility; nature trails; jogging.

RATES: From $59 to $70.

RESERVATIONS: Call (904) 893-2186.

Ponte Vedra Inn & Club

THE ONLY REASON PONTE VEDRA Inn & Club is in the "hidden gems" section is because I've never been there, and I swore that I would include only the resorts I've visited in the first tier. Which is a shame, since everyone (I mean *everyone*) I've spoken to says that the resort's golf courses and spa facilities are among the finest they've experienced. Accommodations rank with the finest, too: All rooms and suites feature designer furniture, ceiling fans, terry robes, separate vanity areas, honor bars and private patios and balconies.

The Ponte Vedra golf courses are very highly regarded. The 6,573-yard Ocean Course was designed by Robert Trent Jones and has water in play on 10 holes in the form of Lake Vedra and its associated lagoons and streams. The shorter Lagoon Course (5,574 yards) by architect Joe Lee has more water in play, but is manageable if played smartly—i.e., leave the driver in the bag on every par-four except the reachable (?) 256-yard second.

Dining, I've been told, is impeccable at the Inn Dining Room and the Seafoam Dining Room, but I've heard that the Golf Club's menu of soups, salads and specialty sandwiches is delightful.

Finally, everyone raves about the 5,000-square-foot oceanfront spa, offering more than 50 beauty and "pampering" services. I wonder...If I were to tell the folks at Ponte Vedra there'll be a second edition of this book...maybe... ■

Ponte Vedra Inn & Club
200 Ponte Vedra Boulevard
Ponte Vedra Beach, FL 32082

LOCATION: 22 miles southeast of Jacksonville, 26 miles north of St. Augustine.

ACCOMMODATIONS: 182 rooms, 20 suites in eight separate low-rise buildings.

DINING/ENTERTAINMENT: Inn Dining Room, Continental cuisine; Seafoam Dining Room, panorama of Atlantic from atop the Surf Club; Florida Room, Casablanca-style with seafood specialties; Golf Club; Surf Club Patio; Audubon Lounge, lobby, cocktails after 5 p.m.; Seahorse Lounge, weekend dancing; High Tides Lounge, beachfront drinks and snacks.

AMENITIES: 36 holes of golf (Robert Trent Jones/Joe Lee); 15 tennis courts (seven lighted); fully equipped fitness center featuring Nautilus equipment and aerobics; oceanfront spa; four swimming pools; fishing; sailing; gift shop and boutique; library; executive business center.

RATES: Call for rates and available golf and spa packages.

RESERVATIONS: Call (800) 327-4960.

Places To Play

Northern Florida

Amelia Island

Summer Beach Resort
4700 Amelia Island Pkwy.
Amelia Island, FL 32034
(904) 261-0624
Type of Facility: Resort
No. of Holes: 18
Design: Marshland
Yardage: 5,039-6,681
Par: 72
Peak Rates: $41.50 for nine, $72.50 for 18. Cart included.

Citrus Springs

Citrus Springs Country Club
8690 Golfview Drive
Citrus Springs, FL 32630
(904) 726-1461
Type of Facility: Semi-private
No. of Holes: 18
Design: Traditional
Yardage: 5,501-6,664
Par: 72
Peak Rates: $28 for 18 holes. Cart included.

Daytona

Pelican Bay Golf & C.C.
350 Pelican Bay Dr.
Daytona, FL 32119
(904) 756-0034
Type of Facility: Semi-private
No. of Holes: 36
Design: Traditional
Yardage: 5,278-6,630
Par: 72
Peak Rates: $30 for 18 holes. Cart included.

Daytona Beach

Indigo Lakes Hilton Resort
2620 Volusia Ave.
Daytona Beach, FL 32114
(904) 258-6333
Type of Facility: Semi-private resort
No. of Holes: 18
Design: Traditional
Yardage: 5,159-7,131
Par: 72
Peak Rates: $46 for 18 holes. Cart included.

Destin

Indian Bayou Golf & C.C.
1 Country Club Road
Destin, FL 32541
(904) 837-6191
TYPE OF FACILITY: Semi-private
NO. OF HOLES: 27
DESIGN: Traditional
YARDAGE: 5,080-7,016
PAR: 72
PEAK RATES: $42 for 18 holes. Cart included.

Seascape Resort & Conf. Center
100 Seascape Drive
Destin, FL 32541
(904) 654-7888
TYPE OF FACILITY: Semi-private
NO. OF HOLES: 18
DESIGN: Links
YARDAGE: 5,415-6,696
PAR: 72
PEAK RATES: From $43 to $52. Cart included.

Fernandina Beach

Fernandina Beach Golf Club
2800 Bill Melton Rd.
Fernandina Beach, FL 32034
(904) 277-7370
TYPE OF FACILITY: Public
NO. OF HOLES: 27
DESIGN: Traditional
YARDAGE: 3,094 (North), 3,709 (West)
PAR: 35 North, 36 South, 37 West
PEAK RATES: $25. Cart included.

Ft. Walton Beach

Ft. Walton Beach Golf Club
Lewis Turner Blvd.
Ft. Walton Beach, FL 32548
(904) 862-3314
TYPE OF FACILITY: Public
NO. OF HOLES: 27
DESIGN: Traditional
YARDAGE: 5,300-6,583
PAR: 72
PEAK RATES: $15. Cart optional.

Gainesville

Ironwood Golf Club
2100 NE 39th Ave.
Gainesville, FL 32609
(904) 334-3120
TYPE OF FACILITY: Public
NO. OF HOLES: 18
DESIGN: Traditional
YARDAGE: 5,700-6,462
PAR: 72
PEAK RATES: $9/12. Cart optional.

Gulf Breeze

The Club at Hidden Creek
3070 PGA Blvd.
Navarre, FL 32566
(904) 939-4604
TYPE OF FACILITY: Semi-private
NO. OF HOLES: 18
DESIGN: Traditional
YARDAGE: 5,206-6,844
PAR: 72
PEAK RATES: $41.50. Cart included.

Jacksonville

Dunes Golf Club
11751 McCormick Road
Jacksonville, FL 32225
(904) 641-8444
TYPE OF FACILITY: Semi-private
NO. OF HOLES: 18
DESIGN: Traditional
YARDAGE: 5,729-6,700
PAR: 72
PEAK RATES: $20/24 for 18 holes. Cart included.

University Country Club
4012 University Blvd. N.
Jacksonville, FL 32211
(904) 744-2124
TYPE OF FACILITY: Semi-private
NO. OF HOLES: 18
DESIGN: Traditional
YARDAGE: 5,587-6,500
PAR: 72
PEAK RATES: $20/25 for 18 holes. Cart included.

Ocala

Golden Ocala Golf & C.C.
7300 U.S. Highway 27 N.W.
Ocala, FL 34482
(904) 629-6229
TYPE OF FACILITY: Public
NO. OF HOLES: 18
DESIGN: Traditional
YARDAGE: 5,591-6,755
PAR: 72
PEAK RATES: $40. Cart included.

Palm Coast

Matanzas Golf Club
398 Lakeview Blvd.
Palm Coast, FL 32157
(904) 446-6330
TYPE OF FACILITY: Semi-private resort
NO. OF HOLES: 18
DESIGN: Traditional
YARDAGE: 5,800-6,985
PAR: 72
PEAK RATES: $42. Cart included.

St. Augustine

Ponce de Leon Resort
4000 U.S. Highway 1 N.
St. Augustine, FL 32095
(904) 829-5314
TYPE OF FACILITY: Semi-private resort
NO. OF HOLES: 18
DESIGN: Traditional
YARDAGE: 5,315-6,878
PAR: 72
PEAK RATES: $57. Cart included.

Tallahassee

Seminole Golf CLub
2550 Pottsdamer Road
Tallahassee, FL 32304
(904) 644-2582
TYPE OF FACILITY: Public
NO. OF HOLES: 18
DESIGN: Traditional
YARDAGE: 5,545-7,033
PAR: 72
PEAK RATES: $25. Cart included.

Central Florida

SO I LIED. NOW THAT WE'RE IN CENTRAL FLORIDA, EVERYTHING I said in the introduction to the Northern segment is to be ignored. Back there I mentioned that I never leave a great resort for which I'm paying good money to search somewhere else for something to occupy my time. That was there. This is here. And there are just too many things to do and see in Central Florida to be ignored. Excursions to Walt Disney World, EPCOT Center, Universal Studios Florida, Marineland, et al., are certainly worth the time and expense...I think. The downside is still the fact that you have to leave resorts of the caliber of Grand Cypress (below) and Grenelefe Resort & Conference Center (below right) to make these excursions. EPCOT and Disney World require a minimum of two days to do them justice, as does Universal Studios. That means to experience the resort *and* the outside attractions to the fullest you'll need at least a week in the area, and unless you're staying at a facility

that provides free transportation to these attractions you'll probably need a rental car too. Unless of course you're driving there anyway, in which case here are some simple directions: Head southeast. This time you'll not only be able to play golf in Georgia and South Carolina, but you can catch a few days at Amelia Island, Palm Coast or Sawgrass while you ease your way down to the middle of the state. Most of the major air carriers fly directly to Orlando International Airport, and most of the area resorts provide transportation from the luggage carousel to their front door without an additional charge. Call your travel agent, naturally, if you intend to fly. And if you are going to drive, by all means call your travel club for the best routes, maps, accommodations and attractions along the way. If you're not yet a member of a travel

club (and if you normally drive more than 10 or 15 miles per day, membership isn't a luxury, it's an investment) you'll probably save enough money on this trip alone to pay two or three years' membership fees. Think about it.

The weather in Central Florida is not really subject to the tropical low-pressure systems that affect the lower southeast portion of the state, or to the Arctic high-pressure systems that are carried by the Jet Stream into the northern region. It may bottom-out at freezing in mid-winter, but those instances are more the extreme exception than the rule. Overall, temperatures—summer and winter—are moderate, with winter nights dropping into the 50s and afternoon highs in the high 60s to mid 70s quite common. It's still Florida, so summer temps can occasionally be uncomfortable, especially with the humidity, but that too is exceptional.

For the most part, Central Florida—along the Atlantic and the Gulf—offers a moderate, semi-tropical climate (which keeps area golf courses in spectacular condition year-round), a wealth of outside attractions and diversions, and, by the way, some of the finest resorts in the Southeast. What else was it that you needed?

DELUXE

Grand Cypress

All this to do, and Nicklaus, too

ON THE GROUNDS OF GRAND Cypress Resort in Orlando, amidst the highly visible, world-renowned art collection which resides there, are stone figures of the Eight Immortals, men, it is said in Chinese mythology, who performed worthy deeds and lived exemplary lives. These figures stand interspersed beside the path on the walk to the Pool Garden, benevolent, compassionate, serene. Which, when you come to think of it, is a pretty nice attitude to take with you on vacation.

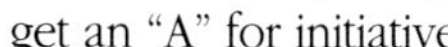

If you happen to leave home without being in the proper frame of mind (whatever you think that is), it is easily found at Grand Cypress, a 1,500-acre resort paradise where you can do as little or as much as you like, be accommodated in luxury either in the private Villas of Grand Cypress or the AAA Five-Diamond Hyatt Regency Grand Cypress, enjoy the international cuisine presented at the resort's 11 restaurants and lounges, and play Jack Nicklaus signature golf. Now, there may not be anything "immortal" about that, but it does sound a lot like dying and going to heaven.

First the golf. I'll admit there aren't many Nicklaus-designed courses I don't like. There aren't *any,* for that matter. But some of Jack's courses, I believe, better reflect the personality of the greatest player ever, and one of those is the New Course at Grand Cypress.

Don't misunderstand. The three nine-hole courses—North, South and East—are great golf courses in their own right, but the New Course has brought much of the tradition and mystique of the Old Course at St. Andrews, Scotland, to this corner of Central Florida, and even if the results weren't as stunning as they truly are, Nicklaus would get an "A" for initiative.

The New Course is what I would expect a Scottish course to look like....on a good day: windswept, dramatic (through its sheer simplicity) in design, and with *loads* of bunkers (there are 145 of them). The knee-high love grass adjacent to—and floating inside—the fairways collects mis-hit shots and refuses to release them, and posting a good score when you're hitting it haywire is improbable. (Okay, *impossible.*)

Nevertheless, if you can find a green or two in regulation, your ball always has a chance of falling in the hole on the moderately undulating putting surfaces. Without getting too far from the equator, playing the New Course is an opportunity to get a feel for the grand old game as it was meant to be played. And you can do it in Bermuda shorts.

The North, South and East courses make you hope Nicklaus will fill up the missing compass point with another classic test of golf. I consider the North course to be the more demanding of the three, but water is in play often throughout the facility, and your ball is never really safe until it finds its way home.

The resort offers a nearly endless array of amenities and activities, from the Grand Cypress Academy of Golf's 3- and 4-day instructional schools, to the Grand Cypress Racquet Club with 12 courts and the comprehensive Tennis Academy, to the Equestrian Center with its 42-stall barn, covered and lighted ring, turn-out paddock, lounge and locker rooms.

Also available is a marina offering windsurfing, sailboats, canoes, rowboats and paddleboats; a health club with Universal weight machines, lifecycles and a stair-climber; croquet; swimming; pitch-and-putt golf; jogging; fitness trail; and bicycle rental. You can really fill up a day here.

Worthy of special mention is Grand Cypress' transportation system (systems, actually). If you are so inclined you can land your helicopter directly on the resort's private helipad (Nice touch!), and once you arrive you can ride the complimentary shuttle that runs between the Hyatt Regency and the Golf Club every 10 minutes. The

Grand Cypress features 45 holes of Jack Nicklaus-designed golf, including the heralded New Course.

resort's trolley service features turn-of-the-century trolleys from Brussels which have been restored and which make the seven-mile trip around the resort with all the appropriate stops every half-hour.

Accommodations are impeccable, be they in the 750-room Hyatt Regency or The Villas of Grand Cypress. The Hyatt offers guest rooms and one- and two-bedroom executive suites. The Villas offer suites with up to four bedrooms and feature oversized baths, living rooms, private patios, dining rooms, private patios or verandahs, fireplace, whirlpool and fully equipped kitchens. The Hyatt features....well, you know what a five-diamond Hyatt Regency features, don't you?

Dining at Grand Cypress is a delight, but choosing a restaurant each evening can be pleasantly difficult. The best advice we can offer is to dine in as many of the restaurants as you can, but be sure to try the Black Swan at The Villas at least once. The brochure says "elegant yet relaxed Continental dining" overlooking the golf course, with the operative word being "elegant."

Finally, one very obvious but often overlooked feature of Grand Cypress Resort is its location. The resort is adjacent to Walt Disney World and EPCOT Center, and other area attractions include Sea World and the Kennedy Space Center. Vacationing next door to the Magic Kingdom affords you the opportunity to actually meet a different "eight immortals," who also "performed worthy deeds and lived exemplary lives." One of them being Snow White. ■

GRAND CYPRESS RESORT
Orlando, Florida

LOCATION: 60 Grand Cypress Boulevard, Orlando, FL 32836; 20 minutes west of Orlando International Airport.

ACCOMMODATIONS: One- to four-bedroom villas at The Villas of Grand Cypress; 750 guest rooms and suites at the Hyatt Regency Grand Cypress.

DINING/ENTERTAINMENT: Eleven restaurants and lounges at the resort including (Hyatt Regency) La Coquina, formal gourmet dining overlooking Lake Windsong; Hemingway's, fresh seafood, steak and game in a Key West atmosphere; Trellises, open daily for cocktails, nightly jazz; Hurricane Bar, in Hemingway's with nightly entertainment; (Villas) Fairways, casual country club setting for breakfast, lunch and dinner; and Black Swan, Continental dining.

AMENITIES: 45 holes of golf (Jack Nicklaus); tennis; racquetball; equestrian; volleyball; all watersports; game room; fitness center.

MEETING FACILITIES: Hyatt Regency: 57,000 square feet of space including Grand Ballroom, exhibit hall and 18 meeting rooms accommodating groups to 3,000. Villas: Executive Meeting Center includes 7,000 square feet in seven meeting and banquet rooms, plus terraces and lakeside settings for groups to 200.

RATES: Villas: from $150 per night in low season to $250 in high season. Hyatt Regency: from $175 per night (low season) to $225 per night (high season).

RESERVATIONS: Call (800) 835-7377.

Innisbrook

The Florida resort where the experience is deja vu all over again

THERE'S AN OLD ADAGE THAT SAYS familiarity breeds contempt. While the sage remains anonymous, we can be sure of two things: 1) The author's "significant other" moved out the day after the ditty was penned, and 2) Whoever is responsible never visited Innisbrook Resort in Tarpon Springs, Fla. If they had, they would realize that familiarity with Innisbrook breeds only a desire to return again and again.

There's something very special about playing golf on a "championship" course (though the term most often has not been used, well, judiciously). The walk down the 18th of Doral's Blue Monster, or The Champion course at PGA National or Pebble Beach, for example, conjures thoughts of four-under-par rounds, in the hunt on the final day, head to head against Couples or Strange, or even Nicklaus or Palmer.

That's the feeling on the tee at Innisbrook's Copperhead course—site each December of the JC Penney Mixed Team Classic—a 7,087-yard beauty that has all the thrills of the championship Florida courses, but with a little something extra: elevation.

Now, don't expect nosebleeds from the altitude (If that's what you're looking for you're better off at Innisbrook's sister resort, Tamarron, in Durango, Colo.), but do expect drastic drops (especially for Florida) and uphill carries and mounding that aid your ball in its quest for its final resting place—the common denominator of Florida golf—the water. The wet stuff is in play on 27 of Innisbrook's 63 holes (although only five of them are on Copperhead), and many of those not so affected have blind shots into the green or bunkering that will make you wish you *were* rolling up your pants legs. (This sounds all too familiar, doesn't it?)

Nevertheless, if played from the regular tees, the Copperhead course may be had. A member of our group during a recent outing shot a three-over-par 74 without hitting very many greens. The secret is in the short game. Copperhead's Bermuda putting surfaces roll fast but very true, and if you reconcile yourself early to the fact that you won't often be getting home in regulation, the course has a propensity for bringing out the smart golfer (however deeply buried in the subconscious that person may be) in all of us.

There's a bit of a respite on the 27-hole Sandpiper course, a 6,245-yard par-

Innisbrook

70 (rating of 69.8), but its lack of length is more than compensated for by its 53 sand bunkers and 12 water hazards. Worthy of special mention are the third hole (Course 1), a 174-yard par-three that plays over water to a double-tiered green, and the sixth (also Course 1), a 550-yard par-five with water left and right and an exceptionally well-protected putting surface.

Then there's the sleeper, the Island course, 6,999 yards of *bad.* Copperhead may occasionally strike at you with its fangs, but this course plays, especially in high winds, like one giant water hazard...with teeth. While it may not be my personal favorite in the state of Florida, or even on the property, the Island course does contain a few of my favorite holes, foremost among them the par-5 seventh. This much-photographed and much-maligned golf hole plays 561 yards dogleg left, with a lake staring you in the face tee to green on the right, and a swamp (with things that go bump in the night) on the left. The course guide says off-handedly that it "may be the most difficult hole on the course." (This *is* beginning to sound familiar, isn't it?) Career shots are required from the tee and the fairway, as the green is elevated and heavily bunkered, but a five on the card at the end of this one is worth a story or two back home.

And the transition upon your return home won't be that difficult, as all of the guest accommodations at Innisbrook are in the form of privately owned condo-

Below: The 561-yard, par-5 seventh hole of the Island course, a stunning (in many ways) dogleg with water to the right and a swamp on the left.

miniums. These 1,000 guest suites—from the partitioned club suites to the 2,000-square-foot, two-bedroom deluxe suites—are contained in 28 low-rise lodges, generously spaced throughout the property and named for famous golf courses around the world. The lodges, golf courses, facilities and all activities are connected by a tram service that passes every point on the property every 15 minutes. Combined with the shuttle service available from Tampa International Airport, this convenient method of transportation means a rental car is truly optional. The service extends to nearby Tarpon Springs, or just about anywhere else you'd care to go, provided reservations are made in advance.

A first-time visitor will be pressed to find time to leave the property, as the amenities package is extensive, and the lounges and restaurants numerous and of high quality.

The Vintage Dining Room at the Island Clubhouse is the most elegant on the property, yet its sophistication is relaxed and unpretentious. I thought it interesting, and flattering, that our server

remembered us on our second visit, nearly two years after our first, and picked right up where he left off with his golf tip "guaranteed" to cure my slicing tee ball. The Vintage is enchanting, romantic, and moderately pricey, but its the perfect way to close out a visit to the resort.

The Copperhead Grille serves per-

INNISBROOK RESORT — PALM HARBOR, FLORIDA

LOCATION: 36750 U.S. Hwy. 19 N., Palm Harbor, FL 34684; 25 miles northwest of Tampa International Airport.

ACCOMMODATIONS: 1,000 guest rooms, all with private balcony or patio, ranging from club suites to two-bedroom deluxe suites.

DINING/ENTERTAINMENT: Vintage Dining Room, classic cuisine, extensive wine list; Copperhead Grille, steaks, chops and ribs; Sandpiper Dining Room, regional seafood.

AMENITIES: 63 holes of golf; 15 tennis courts; six swimming pools; fitness center; fishing; cycling; supervised children's program.

MEETING FACILITIES: 65,000 square feet of function space with 14,000-square-foot exhibition hall; full audio/visual department.

RATES: Accommodations only from $86; golf plans from $109.

RESERVATIONS: Call (800) 456-2000.

haps the best steak east of Amarillo, along with chops and ribs, in a relaxed clubhouse atmosphere adjacent to one of the finest golf courses in Florida. And nightly live entertainment begins at 9 p.m. in the Island Lounge at the Island Clubhouse.

There are a thousand things to do and see, both on the property and off, but of course the most important has to do with a little white ball and a stick. That's why guests visit Innisbrook in the first place, and, not coincidentally, this is where they can either learn the game or fine tune one at one of the premier golf instruction schools in the country, the Golf Institute.

Developed by host professional Jay Overton and run by director of instruction Lew Smither III, the Golf Institute is in operation at Tamarron during the summer and here at Innisbrook in the winter, and features one of the finest instructional staffs in the country.

Smither and his team of teaching professionals offer a student/teacher ratio of only four to one, and that means personalized attention to all aspects of the game—your game—from basics like grip and stance to more advanced concepts like course management. You can increase your distance off the tee, develop a feel for those long irons that seldom leave your golf bag, or shape up a short game that's been keeping your score in the triple-digit range.

In fact, a week or so of golf and golf instruction at Innisbrook will have you more than ready for that "championship" walk up the 18th. Call it a hunch, but there's probably nothing too familiar about that. ■

The Don CeSar A Registry Resort

THE DON CESAR'S STORIED HISTORY dates to 1928, when it was conceived by Thomas Rowe and designed by architect Carlton Beard. The hotel was named after Don Caesar de Bazan, the lead character in the opera "Maritana." (It's a good thing the Three Penny Opera wasn't playing that week, the lead character of that piece being Mack the Knife.) During World War II the Don CeSar was transformed by the government into an Army hospital, then became a Veterans Administration hospital in 1945 and remained so for 25 years.

In 1969 the hotel was abandoned and became a target for vandalism. It appeared the building was headed for utter ruin until a citizens group found a buyer who was willing to renovate the property, at a cost of $3.5 million, and reopen it in 1973. In 1985, a 16-month refurbishment began that would transform the Spanish-themed building into a classical European-style hotel.

Imported Italian marble, crystal chandeliers and more contemporary design themes were incorporated, and with a further renovation in 1991 the resort once again stood proudly as one of the fine old hotels in the U.S. (It is in fact a member of the Historic Hotels of America and is listed on the National Register of Historic Places.)

Today The Don CeSar blends the finest modern amenities with the best Old World service, and offers small though elegantly furnished accommodations in the form of 226 deluxe rooms, 49 luxurious suites and two ultra-exclusive penthouses. All rooms and suites offer views of the Gulf of Mexico or the Intracoastal Waterway, and most include the "standard" amenities you expect like nightly turn-down service, complimentary newspapers, coffee, beach towels, children's programs and the ubiquitous chocolate mint on the pillow.

Although the resort doesn't have its own golf course, it is affiliated with four very fine courses in the immediate area: Isla Del Sol, Bardmoor North, Imperial Lakes and Cypress Creek. A little further on in this book you'll read about Bardmoor, and it comes highly recommended, but the Isla Del Sol course is also a scenic and challenging test that should not be missed.

Only five minutes from the hotel via complimentary shuttle, Isla Del Sol is only 6,266 yards, yet comprises 27 water hazards, 87 bunkers and fairways as narrow as a back-country road. Par-fives are in the neighborhood of 500 yards, par-threes range from 155 yards to about 180, and par-fours peak at around 390. The recommended approach to take is 3-wood, mid-iron, putter. Long off the tee really doesn't matter; short work is the order of the day here.

The Don CeSar features fine dining in the King Charles, the resort's gourmet restaurant serving exquisite Continental fare overlooking the Gulf of Mexico. King Charles is top drawer, as is Zelda's Seafood Cafe, as are all the facilities and amenities at The Don CeSar. And it's a lot nicer having the resort named after a classical opera character than that of, say, a current "popular" vocalist. I don't think Registry Resorts has any desire to manage The Axl Rose. ■

THE DON CESAR — ST. PETERSBURG BEACH, FLA.

LOCATION: 35 miles from Tampa International Airport.

ACCOMMODATIONS: 277 guest rooms including 51 suites and two penthouses.

DINING/ENTERTAINMENT: King Charles, gourmet Continental cuisine overlooking the Gulf; Zelda's Seafood Cafe, indoor/outdoor dining for breakfast, lunch and dinner; Lobby Bar, cocktails and entertainment; Beachcomber Bar & Grill, adjacent to pool and beach for refreshments and snacks.

AMENITIES: Access to four 18-hole golf courses within minutes of the hotel; two all-weather tennis courts (lighted); heated swimming pool; Jacuzzi; watersports including waterskiing, aquabikes and parasailing; biking; complimentary health club.

RATES: Rooms from $115, suites from $205.

RESERVATIONS: Call (813) 360-1881.

Saddlebrook

The Florida resort that's whatever you wish it to be

GOLF WRITER JIM KERR HAS CALLED Saddlebrook resort, located 15 miles north of Tampa, Fla., in tiny Wesley Chapel "the entrance to another world," and "a world-class retreat," but some first-time visitors have difficulty figuring out just where it is they've ended up. Consider the 45 tennis courts (five lighted for night play), and the resident Harry Hopman/Saddlebrook International Tennis, which has produced some of the game's brightest stars including Vitas Gerulaitus, Kathy Rinaldi and fan-favorite *du jour* Jennifer Capriati. Many are tempted to think of Saddlebrook as a "tennis" resort.

Or the fact that the resort comprises some 60,000 square feet of conference facilities that can accommodate groups from 10 to more than 1,000 in ballrooms, boardrooms, banquet rooms and meeting rooms, and that 75 percent of Saddlebrook's guests are of the corporate or group variety. Some are led to believe that Saddlebrook is a "conference" resort.

And with a 270-foot, free-form "Superpool" with 25-meter racing lanes, volleyball net and children's area, as well as a complete fitness center with exercise equipment, steamroom, sauna and massage, fishing in the resort's well-stocked lakes, bicycle and jogging trails, etc., etc., Saddlebrook has many convinced that it is an "activities" resort.

Fortunately, we dyed-in-the-wool golfers realize what is truly important in life, and we're well aware that Saddlebrook's two 18-hole golf courses (one designed by Dean Refram, the other by the King, Arnold Palmer) make Saddlebrook one of the premier "golf" resorts in the state.

Saddlebrook's beginnings in 1974 as a privately owned residential community really gave no indication of what it was to one day become. That area of the state was renowned for its citrus groves and cattle ranching, and at the time there was only one true "resort" in the region, Innisbrook, in nearby Tarpon Springs. A gentleman by the name of Jim Refram (Saddlebrook course architect Dean's father) decided while on a visit to the area that it was the perfect locale for just such a residential

community: small, well-crafted and upscale. Today the Saddlebrook resort is a 480-acre complex of cluster homes and condominiums, with single-family homes tucked in amongst the stands of cypress, pine and palm.

The Saddlebrook course is just what most resort golfers are looking for: enough trouble to make it interesting, enough roll and undulation to make it challenging, and not so long as to make it overbearing. Although the original greens were redesigned by Palmer after the resort was purchased by Penton Publishing in 1979 (and subsequently purchased by Penton's chairman, Tom Dempsey, in 1988), the remainder of the course is much the same as it was nearly 30 years ago.

Playing 6,144 yards to a par of 71, the Saddlebrook course is considered to be flatter, tighter and possibly a bit easier than the Palmer course, although an abundance of trees and water make the appraisal subjective, at least. And if the course is just *too* easy for your game you can always walk back to the blue tees, where the distance increases to 6,603 yards and holes like the 448-yard, par-4 seventh—with its fairway bunkers in the landing area and a putting surface surrounded on three sides by water—will get your perspective back in tune with reality, pronto.

The 425-yard, par-four 18th is regarded by many as one of the prettiest finishing holes in the 25-course county. A dogleg right with an "island" of landing area amid a cluster of fairway bunk-

Saddlebrook's Superpool features 25-meter racing lanes, a water volleyball net and a children's area.

ers, the hole requires imagination and patience. The temptation is to crush one off the tee and let it fade into the fairway, but an overzealous whack can easily reach the bunkering right or the water just ahead, and the bunkering left is in perfect position to swallow a slight draw. Think *3-wood* when playing Saddlebrook, especially on 18. And think *left* at all times: Water is in play on the right side of 12 of Saddlebrook's holes; on the left only seven.

The Palmer course offers a little more of everything: more length (6,469 yards from the back tees, although only 6,044 up front); more water (incredibly, in play on every hole except the 510-yard, par-five 11th); more tight, twisting doglegs (hitting your ball sideways is sometimes a blessing in disguise); and more marquee value (Hey! He's the King). It also has a rarity these days—a par-three finishing hole. At only 148 yards, the feeling on the tee of No. 18 is "very possible two, slam-dunk three." But with water front and right, bunkers left and right and a green about as wide as a walk-in closet, it really isn't over 'til you know when.

From either of these two fine courses it's a chip shot to the Walking Village, where shops, restaurants, the pool and some of the guest quarters are centrally located. That's where you'll be exposed to the diverse groups currently visiting Saddlebrook—tennis buffs, conference attendees, fitness fanatics. But you'll always be able to tell which are the golfers. When you say that one of the resort's courses was designed by the King, they'll be the ones who know you *don't* mean Elvis Presley. ■

SADDLEBROOK
Wesley Chapel, Florida

LOCATION: 5700 Saddlebrook Way, Wesley Chapel, FL 33543; approximately 33 miles north of Tampa International Airport.

ACCOMMODATIONS: 500 rooms and condominiums, including one-, two- and three-bedroom suites with full kitchens.

DINING/ENTERTAINMENT: The Cypress Room, casual elegance and moderate prices, American and Continental cuisine; The Little Club, beef, poultry and seafood with a lounge and greenhouse; The Little Club Patio, open-air breakfast, lunch and snacks; the Snack Shack; the Polo Lounge, three-tiered lounge adjacent to Cypress Room with entertainment and dancing nightly; the Superpool Bar; room service 6:30 a.m. to 11 p.m.

AMENITIES: 36 holes of golf (Dean Refram, Arnold Palmer); 45 tennis courts, five lighted for night play; instruction at Harry Hopman/Saddlebrook International Tennis; large free-form Superpool; fitness center with sauna, whirlpool, steam rooms, massage and hair salon for men and women; fishing; 45 minutes from Gulf of Mexico beaches; 15 min. from Busch Gardens, 70 min. from Disney World.

MEETING FACILITIES: More than 60,000 square feet of space, including the 12,500-square-foot Royal Palm Ballroom with seating for 1,800 theatre style, 1,150 for banquets.

RATES: Deluxe rooms from $90 to $175; suites from $105 to $325.

RESERVATIONS: Call (800) 729-8383 or (813) 973-1111.

Marriott's Orlando World Center

ONE MARVELS AT MARRIOTT'S penchant for matching the right golf course designer to the right property. The Orlando World Center, for example, is the largest resort in the state, and as such draws a heavy conference/convention clientele. Marriott chose Joe Lee, one of the true masters of Florida golf course design, to construct a challenging yet fair layout that would keep the low handicappers *very* interested, while not browbeating first-time or apprentice players into submission. (I'll bet someone draws a six-figure annual salary for making these decisions, don't you think?)

In any case, Lee has fashioned an 18-hole masterpiece of simplicity here, a 6,272-yard, par-71 track with a slope rating of 127.4 from the championship tees; eminently playable for the weekend swinger, exceptionally testing for the above-average golfer.

The course is sited on more than 130 acres of the 200-acre property, and winds around and past the 27-story hotel on three sides, making nearly every one of the 1,503 rooms (that's not a typo) a golf view. With water in play on 15 holes and a total of 85 sand bunkers, each shot must be carefully planned and executed (so what's new?) if a decent score (especially from the tips) is to be carded. Tree-lined fairways, rockscapes, bridges and pot bunkering add dimension to the challenge, and tight doglegs and infuriating pin positions on the medium-sized greens complicate matters even further.

But it remains a course that can be played in four hours or less, which for many is important in this neck of the woods, considering the world-renown attractions available in the immediate area like the Magic Kingdom, EPCOT Center, Cypress Gardens, Spaceport U.S.A. and Sea World.

Another *extra* you can always count on at a Marriott resort is the "newness" of the accommodations. Indeed, in 1991 when the resort was but five years old, Marriott poured $11 million into renovation and redecoration of all 1,503 (it's *still* not a typo) guest lodgings, giving them new carpets, draperies, bedspreads and paint.

In the hotel proper they've added more tropical plants and landscaping to the already botanical garden-like setting, such as Sabal palm, banana trees and jade plants, bringing the total plantings on property to over 5,600 pieces. There are 13 water features (not counting the golf course) including fountains and

MARRIOTT'S ORLANDO WORLD CENTER

LOCATION: 8701 World Center Drive, Orlando, FL 32821; 5 minutes from EPCOT.

ACCOMMODATIONS: 1,503 guest rooms including 101 suites and 100 concierge-level rooms with additional amenities.

DINING/ENTERTAINMENT: Mikado Japanese Steak House; Garden Terrace, family dining; Regent Court, gourmet dining in elegant atmosphere; Golf Grille, casual with lighted fare; Stachio's, indoor snack bar and video games; Palm's, poolside snack bar; Regent Court Lounge; Pavillion, poolside lounge; Pagoda Lounge, lobby piano bar.

AMENITIES: 18 holes of golf (Joe Lee); 12 tennis courts (lighted); four swimming pools including a 17,000-square-foot main pool; locker rooms with sauna for men and women; four whirlpools; fully equipped health club with Universal and free weights, massage, stationary bikes and Stairmaster; five-acre activity court with pools, waterslide, restaurants and lounges; five gift shops; beauty and barber shop; photography services; car rental; local tours and attraction tickets.

MEETING FACILITIES: More than 143,000 square feet of flexible space including two 40,000-square-foot ballrooms, exhibition hall, 14 meeting rooms and three executive conference suites.

RATES: Deluxe rooms from $210; suites from $250 to $670.

RESERVATIONS: Call (800) 621-0638 or (407) 239-4200.

waterfalls, and 13 man-made lakes. (Do you get the feeling you need webbed feet to get around here?)

Dining at Orlando World Center runs the gamut from fast food to sophisticated. The Garden Terrace offers fabulous buffets, but you'll be dining with other families' children, if you know what I mean. Couples are better served in the elegant Regent Court, with great service and a complete wine list to boot. With 10 restaurants and lounges on property—including the famous Mikado Japanese Steak House and the uncrowded Golf Grille—you're sure to find *something* to suit your taste.

Included in the hotel's function space are the 40,000-square-foot Grand and Crystal Ballrooms and the 51,000-square-foot Palms Exhibition Hall, three of the largest conference and convention facilities in the state. The oversized pre-function area features gardens, fountains and sky-lights, and the entire area is resplendent in Italian marble.

A few last words on accommodations: While standard rooms are much more than adequate, the 100 concierge-level rooms on the 11th and 12th floors come with honor bar and complimentary breakfast and afternoon buffet. A private elevator (one of 27) speeds you to a waiting concierge who will arrange transportation to the area's activities, make restaurant reservations and fulfill any other special requests.

Marriott is known world-wide for its service, and no finer example of that commitment can be found than the Orlando World Center. I'm sure someone else draws a six-figure salary making sure that will always be the case. ■

Bardmoor

Largo's "upscale" public golf course

I'VE SEEN THE WORD "UPSCALE" USED too many ways too many times to feel comfortable around it. It's usually just a polite way of saying It Costs More Money. Now *that* I understand.

But I also understand the concept of the formation of upscale public golf courses such as Bardmoor North Golf Club in Largo. The thinking behind it is pretty sound: That golfers who can afford to pay more to play than the average are willing to part with their money more readily if they're treated like club members on the day they play. It works just fine on Hilton Head at Hilton Head National, and it works just fine at Bardmoor.

There are no amenities, save the new, functional clubhouse with its restaurant and lounge and a stunning new practice facility designed by Tom Fazio, unless you count the "player's assistant" who cruises the course with sleeves of balls and a cellular phone. There is bag drop-off service and club cleaning after the round, and there are instructional clinics and individual lessons by PGA certified professionals. Okay, okay, there are also new range balls (at all times) and a new fleet of golf carts. But I'm not going to spend More Money for things like that. I *am* going to spend More Money for 18 holes of straightaway, championship-caliber golf, and that is the main attraction here. In fact, Bardmoor was once the site of the JCPenney Classic, now contested on the Copperhead course at Innisbrook Resort near Tarpon Springs.

Playing a sturdy 6,960 yards from the blue tees (6,484 white, 5,569 red), the course features 10 holes with water directly in play, two par-threes of over 190 yards and a rip-roaring finishing hole, the 573-yard, par-five 18th.

Eighteen has water running the left side from tee to fairway (which itself is a pretty good poke), then funnels into a tree- and bunker-lined tube that leaves absolutely no margin for error. The putting surface is well protected and moderately undulating, providing a great place to settle the afternoon's wagers. And you know what that means: More Money. ■

For information call (813) 397-0483.

Grand Harbour Golf & Beach Club

EVERY PICTURE INDEED TELLS A story, and you'll get an ear full at Grand Harbor Golf & Beach Club in Vero Beach, one of the most uncrowded and unspoiled areas in the southeastern U.S. The country club lifestyle enjoyed by property owners at Grand Harbor is available to resort guests through a rental program, and included in the amenities are two fine golf courses, the Harbor designed by Pete Dye and River by Joe Lee.

Though both courses are small (River, 6,253 yards; Harbor, 5,746) they nevertheless offer the usual Dye/Lee trademarks such as lakeside bulkheading, deep pot bunkers and rolling fairways from Dye, and marshland magic from hole routing through estuaries, wildlife habitats and aquatic preserves from Lee.

The resort lodgings are a great value if you consider the monthly rental rates of $3,000 to $5,000 (off-season rates are about half, and weekly rates are available) provide membership in Grand Harbor Club, with green fees included. The Mediterranean-theme residences and resort buildings are exquisitely crafted, and the secluded oceanfront beach club is straight out of "Lifestyles of the Rich and Famous." But don't take my word for it, *listen* to the pictures. ■

For information call (800) 826-8293.

Grenelefe Resort

"LET'S TAKE A MEETING" BECAME A popular phrase in the 1980s, and if you're shopping around for a place to take one in the '90s you need look no further than Grenelefe Resort & Conference Center near Orlando. With a voluminous 70,000 square feet of flexible meeting facilities available—including a grand ballroom that seats over 1,500 for banquets and a business center with fax, computer, and shipping services—corporations such as Sony, USAir, Delta and Unisys have found Grenelefe to be the perfect location for getting down to business. Of course, the fact that Grenelefe offers 54 holes of superlative golf, tennis, a marina and exquisite dining probably has nothing at all to do with it.

But whether you're traveling with a group of four or 400, Grenelefe is a place you'll want to visit. The resort's 7,325-yard West Course—built in 1965 by David Wallace from a preliminary routing plan by Robert Trent Jones—has been ranked among the 10 best in the state of Florida. The East Course, at 6,802 yards, is an Ed Seay design from the mid-1970s that features a first-hole championship tee sited on the second story of the Conference Center. Its tight, tree-lined fairways place a premium on accuracy off the tee. The par-71 South Course is Grenelefe's latest addition, a Ron Garl/Andy Bean layout incorporating many links-style design elements including extensive mounding and bunkering and an abundance of water.

With the resort's largest restaurant, Camelot, overlooking the South Course, *apres* golf you can apply yourself to the second most popular phrase of the business-oriented '80s: Let's do lunch. ■

Grenelefe Resort & Conf. Center
3200 State Road 546
Grenelefe, FL 33844

LOCATION: 30 minutes south of Walt Disney World, 45 minutes from Orlando Int'l. Airport.

ACCOMMODATIONS: 950 deluxe one- and two-bedroom condominiums and villas.

DINING/ENTERTAINMENT: Grene Heron, elegant European-style menu and service; Camelot, casual breakfast, lunch and dinner; West Clubhouse Forest Pub, Continental breakfast, cocktails and sandwiches; poolside snack bar; Lancelot's Lounge, entertainment.

AMENITIES: Three 18-hole golf courses; 20 tennis courts (11 lighted for night play); full-service marina and boating on Lake Marion; four swimming pools; miniature golf; nature trails; bicycle rental; convenience store; game room; beauty salon.

MEETING FACILITIES: 70,000 square feet of meeting and exhibit space accommodating groups to 2,000.

RATES: Variety of golf packages available from $99 to $179.

RESERVATIONS: Call (813) 422-7511.

Walt Disney World

FOR THOSE OF YOU WHO THINK golf at Walt Disney World is (excuse me for this) Mickey Mouse, let me tell you, that opinion is downright Goofy, especially with the recent addition of Pete Dye's Eagle Pines course and Tom Fazio's Osprey Ridge to the existing three courses—Palm, Magnolia and Lake Buena Vista—designed by Joe Lee.

Fairways of the 6,772-yard Eagle Pines are exceptionally wide and dished rather than crowned, which often steers errant shots away from hazards and back into play. The most unusual aspect of the course is the absence of rough. Dye bordered the fairways with pinestraw, which not only tends to reward mis-hit shots with more forgiving lies but lends an appealing aesthetic quality to the layout.

Fazio's Osprey Ridge (like Eagle Pines) successfully accommodates golfers of varying ability levels with tees set from 5,402 to 7,101 yards. The greens are fast-rolling and mildly undulating, and extensive mounding (some man made, some not) is a factor on most of the holes. Osprey Ridge is considered by many to be the more scenic of the two, and the easier course on which to score well. These two new courses, and the Lee-designed gems that have been around for some time now, make golf at Walt Disney World an activity rather than an amenity. Golf here is no longer just a walk in the, ah, *theme* park. ■

Walt Disney World Resort
Orlando, Florida

ACCOMMODATIONS: Seventeen hotels, a campground and vacation villas.

DINING/ENTERTAINMENT: An array of fine restaurants in all of the hotels and in the surrounding Orlando area.

RECREATION: Five 18-hole golf courses and a nine-hole family facility; Typhoon Lagoon water theme park; River Country water park; Discovery Island tropical gardens and zoological park; tennis courts; pools and lakes for swimming, boating, waterskiing and fishing; jogging paths; horseback riding.

ATTRACTIONS: Magic Kingdom, EPCOT Center, Disney MGM Studios/Theme Park, Pleasure Island nightclub theme park, Disney Village marketplace with more than two dozen shops and restaurants

RATES: Value seasons for most accommodations are Jan. 5 to Feb. 8, April 26 to June 6 and Aug. 16 to Dec. 19. Theme parks, golf courses and attractions have year-round rates.

INFORMATION: Call (407) 824-4321.

Places To Play

Central Florida

Apollo Beach

Apollo Beach Golf & Sea Club
801 Golf & Sea Blvd.
Apollo Beach, FL 33572
(813) 645-6212
Type of Facility: Public
No. of Holes: 18
Design: Traditional
Yardage: 5,300-7,150
Par: 72
Peak Rates: $30 for 18 holes. Cart included.

Bartow

Bartow Golf Club
150 Idlewood Ave.
Bartow, FL 33830
(813) 533-9183
Type of Facility: Public
No. of Holes: 18
Design: Traditional
Yardage: 5,400-6,300
Par: 72
Peak Rates: $9.50 for 18 holes. Cart $8.50.

Bradenton

Manatee County Golf Club
6415 53rd Ave. W.
Bradenton, FL 34210
(813) 792-6773
Type of Facility: Public
No. of Holes: 18
Design: Traditional
Yardage: 5,619-6,747
Par: 72
Peak Rates: Vary by season. Call for rates.

Palma Sola Golf Club
3807 75th Street W.
Bradenton, FL 34209
(813) 792-7476
Type of Facility: Public
No. of Holes: 18
Design: Traditional
Yardage: 5,900-6,300
Par: 72
Peak Rates: Call for rates.
Comments: Close to beaches.

Clearwater

Clearwater Country Club
525 N. Betty Lane
Clearwater, FL 34615
(813) 443-5078
TYPE OF FACILITY: Semi-private
NO. OF HOLES: 18
DESIGN: Traditional
YARDAGE: 5,700-6,300
PAR: 72
PEAK RATES: $35 for 18 holes. Cart included.

Belleview Mido Resort Hotel
1501 Indian Rocks Road
Belle Air, FL 34616
(813) 581-5498
TYPE OF FACILITY: Semi-private resort
NO. OF HOLES: 18
DESIGN: Traditional
YARDAGE: 5,601-6,550
PAR: 72 (74 Women)
PEAK RATES: $55 for 18 holes. Cart included.

Cocoa Beach

Cocoa Beach Country Club
5000 Tom Warriner Blvd.
Cocoa Beach, FL 32931
(407) 868-3351
TYPE OF FACILITY: Public
NO. OF HOLES: 27
DESIGN: Links
YARDAGE: From 3,021 to 3,349
PAR: 35/36/36
PEAK RATES: $28. $7.50 1/2 cart.

Debary

Glen Abbey Golf Club
391 N. Pine Meadow Dr.
Debary, FL 32713
(407) 668-4209
TYPE OF FACILITY: Semi-private
NO. OF HOLES: 18
DESIGN: Traditional
YARDAGE: 5,410-6,629
PAR: 72
PEAK RATES: $29/31. Cart included.

Deland

Saulteridge
800 E. Euclid Ave.
Deland, FL 32724
(904) 736-0560
TYPE OF FACILITY: Public
NO. OF HOLES: 18
DESIGN: Traditional
YARDAGE: 5,599-6,111
PAR: 72
PEAK RATES: $14. Cart optional.

Deltona

Deltona Hills Golf & C.C.
1120 Elkcam Blvd.
Deltona, FL 32725
(904) 789-4911
TYPE OF FACILITY: Semi-private
NO. OF HOLES: 18
DESIGN: Traditional
YARDAGE: 5,882-6,841
PAR: 72, Women 73.
PEAK RATES: $27. Cart included.

Dunedin

Dunedin Country Club
1050 Palm Blvd.
Dunedin, FL 34698
(813) 733-7836
Type of Facility: Semi-private
No. of Holes: 18
Design: Traditional
Yardage: 5,726-6,565
Par: 72, Women 73.
Peak Rates: $38 for 18 holes. Cart included.

Howie-in-the-Hills

Mission Inn Resort
10400 CR 48
Howie-in-the-Hills, FL 34737
(904) 324-3101
Type of Facility: Resort
No. of Holes: 36
Design: Traditional/Links
Yardage: 6,814/6,820
Par: 72/72
Peak Rates: $75 for 18 holes. Cart included.

Indian Lake Estates

Indian Lake Estates Golf & C.C.
Red Grange Ave.
Indian Lake Estates, FL 33855
(813) 692-1514
Type of Facility: Semi-private
No. of Holes: 18
Design: Traditional
Yardage: 5,157-6,413
Par: 72
Peak Rates: $22. Cart optional.

Inverness

Inverness Golf & Country Club
3150 Country Club Dr.
Inverness, FL 34450
(904) 726-2583
Type of Facility: Semi-private
No. of Holes: 18
Design: Traditional
Yardage: 5,354-6,265
Par: 72
Peak Rates: $25. Cart included.

Kissimmee

Orange Lake Country Club
8505 W. Irlo Bronson Mem. Hwy.
Kissimmee, FL 34746
(800) 877-6522
Type of Facility: Public (Timeshare)
No. of Holes: 27
Design: Traditional
Yardage: 3,216/3,332/3,335
Par: 36/36/36
Peak Rates: $52. Cart included.

Lake Placid

Placid Lakes Inn & Golf Club
3601 Jefferson Ave.
Lake Placid, FL 33852
(813) 465-4333
Type of Facility: Semi-private
No. of Holes: 18
Design: Links
Yardage: 5,312-6,549
Par: 72
Peak Rates: $20. Cart included.

Lakeland

Sandpiper Golf & C.C.
6001 Sandpiper Dr.
Lakeland, FL 33809
(813) 859-5461
Type of Facility: Semi-private
No. of Holes: 18
Design: Links
Yardage: 5,024-6,500
Par: 70
Peak Rates: $18 for 18 holes. Cart included.

Largo

Bayou Club
7979 Bayou Club Blvd.
Largo, FL 34647
(813) 399-1000
Type of Facility: Semi-private
No. of Holes: 18
Design: Traditional
Yardage: 7,054
Par: 72
Peak Rates: Guest rate available.
Comments: Tom Fazio design.

Melbourne

Harbor City Municipal G.C.
2750 Lake Washington Rd.
Melbourne, FL 32935
(407) 255-4606
Type of Facility: Public
No. of Holes: 18
Design: Traditional
Yardage: 5,399-6,955
Par: 71
Peak Rates: Call for rates.

Melbourne Beach

Spessard Holland Golf Course
2374 Oak St.
Melbourne Beach, FL 32951
(407) 952-4529
Type of Facility: Public
No. of Holes: 18
Design: Traditional
Yardage: 3,959-5,065
Par: 67
Peak Rates: $20. Cart optional.

New Port Richey

Magnolia Valley Golf Club
7223 Massachusetts Ave.
New Port Richey, FL 34653
(813) 847-2342
Type of Facility: Semi-private
No. of Holes: 27
Design: Marshland
Yardage: 4,880-6,200
Par: 71
Peak Rates: $20. Cart included.

New Smyrna Beach

New Smyrna Beach Golf Club
1000 Wayne Ave.
New Smyrna Beach, FL 32168
(904) 427-3437
Type of Facility: Public
No. of Holes: 18
Design: Traditional
Yardage: 5,500-6,400
Par: 72
Peak Rates: $23.50. Cart included.

Orlando

Dubsdread Golf Club
549 W. Pan
Orlando, FL 32804
(407) 246-2551
Type of Facility: Public
No. of Holes: 18
Design: Traditional
Yardage: 5,575-6,055
Par: 71
Peak Rates: $25 for 18 holes. Cart included.

Hunters Creek Golf Club
14401 Sports Club Way
Orlando, FL 32387
(407) 240-4653
Type of Facility: Public
No. of Holes: 18
Design: Traditional
Yardage: 5,755-7,432
Par: 72
Peak Rates: $50 for 18 holes. Cart included.

Sebring

Sun 'n Lake Golf & C.C.
5200 Sun 'n Lake Blvd.
Sebring, FL 33872
(813) 385-4830
Type of Facility: Semi-private resort
No. of Holes: 27
Design: Nine traditional, 18 Links
Yardage: 5,029/6,742
Par: 36/36/36
Peak Rates: $32. Cart included.

St. Petersburg

Mangrove Bay Golf Club
875 62nd Ave. N.E.
St. Petersburg, FL 33702
(813) 893-7797
Type of Facility: Public
No. of Holes: 18
Design: Traditional
Yardage: 5,172-6,779
Par: 72
Peak Rates: $27. Cart included.

Titusville

Bent Oak Golf & C.C.
4304 Londontown Rd.
Titusville, FL 32796
(407) 383-1234
Type of Facility: Semi-private
No. of Holes: 18
Design: Traditional
Yardage: 5,808/6,600
Par: 71
Peak Rates: $28 includes 1/2 cart.

Wildwood

Rolling Hills Country Club
Rt. 2 Box 180
Wildwood, FL 34785
(904) 748-4200
Type of Facility: Semi-private
No. of Holes: 18
Design: Traditional
Yardage: 5,449-6,509
Par: 71, Women 72.
Peak Rates: $24.40. Cart included.

Southern Florida

LET'S GET THE BASICS OUT OF THE WAY FORTHWITH. FIRST, YOU know my best advice is to contact your travel consultant if you intend to fly to Southern Florida, and your travel club if you intend to drive. Really, don't leave home without them.

Second, let's not kid ourselves about South Florida weather. During the winter months it's gorgeous (which is why you'll pay top dollar for your vacation), with temperatures in the mid to upper 80s (falling into the 70s at night) and the chance of rain exceptionally slim. During the summer it's, well, it's the reason you get such great deals at the area's best resorts. Temperatures are often in the high 90s with humidity to match. Some days the sun just hammers you, making mid-day golf or tennis an outing only for the hearty, or the fool-hardy. Nevertheless, if you schedule your outdoor activities for early morning and late afternoon and keep yourself occupied indoors during the heat of the day, you can really cash in on the fantastic deals and packages seemingly every resort now offers. (The rates included at the end of each section are usually the lowest off-season rate available. Don't be surprised if you call in December and find them two or three times higher.)

Two of the best times to travel to Southern Florida are early fall and late spring; the former before the resorts raise their rates for the high season, the latter after the rates have been lowered but prior to the onset of full summer. Of course the hurricane season is a factor from mid summer through November, so you run the risk of heavy rains, at least, and there have been a few South Florida spring showers that have gone on indefinitely, so there's always a chance something will go wrong weatherwise.

Ironically, Southern Florida has more of the outside activities that I enjoy than any other area of the state. It's ironic because four of my personal top-10 resorts are in this region, and you know how I feel about leaving the properties. But with the Miami Dolphins of the NFL, the Miami Heat of the NBA and the National League's Miami Marlins (I'm not sure, but I think by now the braintrust that schedules these sports has the seasons of all three overlapping), it's difficult not to catch a game while you're in town. There are the gardens and Miznerесque architecture of Vizcaya, the Planetarium in northern Coconut Grove, shopping in Palm Beach and Ft. Lauderdale, the trip via Alligator Alley through Everglades National Park, the revitalized South Beach area of Miami Beach, the fine dining in Coral Gables, the shelling extraordinaire on Sanibel Island and the adventure of the Florida Keys. If you must go somewhere, these are all pretty good places to start. The concierge at your hotel will be happy to recommend countless others and in most cases will make all the arrangements necessary.

But it will be difficult to tear yourself away from the golf at Palm Beach Polo (left) or the stunning accommodations of The Breakers (above) or the Blue Monster at Doral or The Champion course at PGA National. You also must contend with luxurious amenities such as the spas at Doral, Palm-Aire or Bonaventure (below). When you first experience the facilities and services at these fine resort spas, you'll wonder why it's taken you so long to try them. You'll be pampered, beautified, worked-out, made over and sent home a completely different person than the one that checked in. You'll suffer the fate of the weekend duffer on the difficult course at Marco Island, but possibly shoot even par or better on the West course at Bonaventure in return. You'll be treated like royalty at Turnberry Isle, be massaged into mindlessness at The Inverrary, and discover at Don Shula's Hotel & Golf Club that some of the best golf courses in the state are considerably lesser known than others.

One recent national golf publication called Florida "one long fairway with water on both sides," which is about the most accurate description of golf in the state I've ever heard. The game may not have originated here, but there's certainly no better place to play it (except, of course, the Bahamas and the Caribbean).

The diversity of Florida layouts is mind-boggling, considering that 90 percent of the state is, it seems, at or below sea level. There are links courses, traditional courses, marshland courses, parkland, oceanside, lakeside and (unbelievably) hillside courses, all of which are waiting for you and your sticks and a sleeve or two (or possibly three) of balls. If you've never been to Southern Florida, you're in for the golf vacation of your life. If you have, you know what I'm talking about.

Make the time. Find the money. Call your travel agent....And get a move on.

Boca Raton Resort & Club

Where Gatsby, or Redford, would feel right at home

REMEMBER THAT SCENE IN THE movie *The Great Gatsby*, where Robert Redford as Jay Gatsby stands alone outside his estate house, resplendent in his dinner jacket, privately, silently bemoaning the excess with which he is surrounded? You had to feel for the guy—a victim of his own circumstance, a quiet, uncharacteristically simple man trapped by his station in life.

Yo! Gatsmo. *Go with it*, babe.

I've thought of Redford, er, Gatsby, in that very position every time I've been lucky enough to stand anywhere on the property of the Boca Raton Resort & Club, the Addison Mizner-designed "palace in paradise."

The storied history of this resort begins during the same period when those real-life incarnations of the Gatsby character were frequenting South Florida primarily as a curative for their ailing minds and bodies. The rigors of living "up North," and the sheer misery that is apparently attached to extreme wealth were taking their toll on these societal stalwarts, and the exodus began in earnest after eccentric architect Mizner met eccentric industrialist Singer (Paris, that is, of sewing machine fame), both of whom were convinced they had but months to live. First the two designed and built the Everglades Club in Palm Beach. When Mizner realized he would be around a bit longer than he had initially anticipated he began designing some of those famous South Florida mansions.

But Mizner's dream (appropriately, *Mizner's Dream* is the name of the yacht that shuttles guests back and forth between The Cloister and the Beach Club) was to build "the greatest resort in the world," and after purchasing more than 17,000 acres of Boca Raton real estate he designed and built The Cloister Inn in 1926, the anchor property in the grand design.

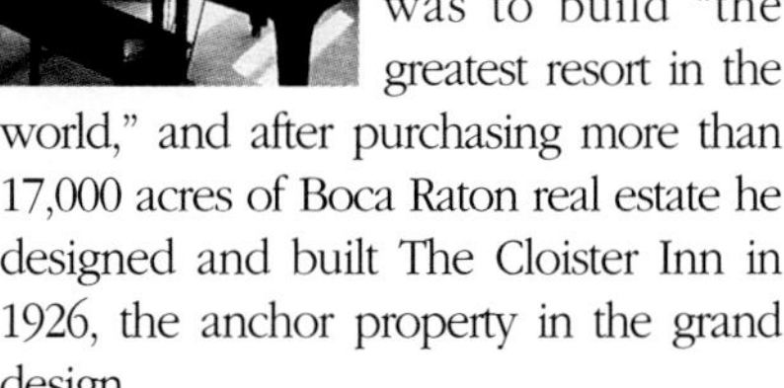

The Cloister is an exceptionally imaginative Spanish-Mediterranean/Moorish structure with hidden gardens, barrel-tile roofs and ornate fountains, and furnished with rare antiques from Spain and Central America. It immediately drew the likes of the du Ponts, Vanderbilts, Ziegfelds and Ardens. The splendor of their northern estates had been magically transported to the sunny South Florida coast.

In essence, that is what the Boca Raton Resort & Club has remained these past sixty-something years. There have been a number of ownership changes in that time, and it seems as though the property is in a constant state of renovation and upgrading (to the tune of $11 million in 1991 alone), but basically the dream of Addison Mizner has been left intact. Enhanced and modernized, granted, but intact.

Golf arrived at the Boca Raton Resort & Club in 1926 when William Flynn designed a relatively flat, semi-remarkable layout—as good as could be expected given the near featureless terrain and the limitations of resort-course golf. Tommy Armour was the resident professional here for 29 years, and in 1956, when Sam Snead replaced Armour as the pro, Robert Trent Jones made changes to the original design. Major reconstruction of the course took place in 1988 under the auspices of golf architect Joe Lee, who reshaped the three existing lakes and added another, among other things.

The net result is a very playable resort course, yet one that is challenging enough from the back tees (6,682 yards, par-71) to keep the interest of the low-handicap golfer.

The green of the 512-yard, par-five 18th at Boca Country Club, where water is in play on 15 holes.

The course begins rather quietly with a straightaway par-four of 387 yards—no excuses for anything more than par here—but starts making noise on No. 2, a short but devastatingly tight dogleg left, where the tee shot requires head-of-a-pin precision to the middle of the landing area about 215 to 225 yards out. No advantage is taken from blistering a drive; instead, a 3-wood in position for a 100- to 110-yard wedge shot, over water, is the way to go.

Conversely, the third hole demands a crushed drive, as this dogleg-right par-four stretches to 398 yards and features bunkering to the left and right of the normal landing zone. Short and right here makes a guaranteed six (and *at least* one shot from a fairway or green-side bunker). Long and left can turn into a three if you reach the green in regulation; the putting surfaces are well manicured and roll very, very true.

Water isn't in play again until No. 9, a monstrous par-five of nearly 600 yards that requires three exacting shots, the first two down the extreme right-hand side of the fairway. I've never heard of an eagle being made here; I'm not sure it's possible, considering the requirements: 1) two 300-yard shots (one off the fairway) and a putt, or 2) an unbelievably lucky hole-out from about 120-yards away. My guess is the chances are better for the latter, with as much regularity as being struck by a meteor.

The homeward nine is bookended by two fine holes, the 553-yard, par-five 10th and the 445-yard, par-four 18th. No. 10 isn't tricked up or wet or sandy; in fact, you have to look for trouble to find it. What it offers is the chance to hit four

Boca Raton Resort & Club
Boca Raton, Florida

LOCATION: 501 East Camino Real, Boca Raton, FL 33431; 28 miles south of Palm Beach Airport; 24 miles north of Fort Lauderdale International Airport.

ACCOMMODATIONS: The Cloister: 338 deluxe rooms; 48 concierge-level rooms and suites in the Palm Court Club. The Tower: 242 deluxe rooms including 76 studios and seven suites. Boca Beach Club: 214 rooms including nine suites. Golf Villas: 120 rooms overlooking the golf course

DINING/ENTERTAINMENT: Top of the Tower The Italian Restaurant, authentic Italian cuisine, dinner only; Nick's Fishmarket, seafood from around the world; The Patio; Chauncey's Court; The Cabana; Garden Grille; Cappy's Bar; Gazebo Bar; Island Bar; El Lago Lounge; Halfway House.

AMENITIES: 36 holes of golf; 34 tennis courts (nine lighted for night play); five swimming pools; water sports including windsurfing, sailing, parasailing and snorkeling; children's activities program; three fitness centers; bicycling; croquet; badminton; walking tours of the gardens; racquetball at Boca Country Club. Full-service marina (23 slips) at Mile Marker 67, Intracoastal Waterway.

MEETING FACILITIES: More than 70,000 square feet of space (31 rooms) accommodating 10 to 1,500.

RATES: Deluxe rooms from $115 to $400; suites from $210 to $3,000.

RESERVATIONS: Call (800) 327-0101 or (407) 395-3000.

solid golf shots and make birdie. Likewise on 18, long enough to force you to "juice it" a little, but a real opportunity to close out the day on a positive note.

Whereas the par-fours and fives on the resort course are the main attractions, the strength of the Country Club course is in its par-threes, two of which hover in the 190-yard range, and one, the 128-yard 13th, that shouldn't be considered a pushover until you've carded your score.

Regardless of where you play that day, or how, you can take solace in the fact that you'll be returning to your guest quarters in either The Tower, The Cloister or (my personal favorite) the Beach Club. Accommodations are truly spectacular in all three, helping to win for the resort the coveted Mobil Five-Star and AAA Five-Diamond awards for the past kazillion years.

Naturally, dining is an experience to be savored, whether at Chauncey's Court with its informal setting and its equally informal menu, or at the Top of The Tower, with its abnormally magnificent views and very formal atmosphere. (Guess which one I prefer.)

So there I was, on the last night of my most recent visit to the resort, in one of the secluded gardens behind The Cloister, daydreaming myself into the role of Jay Gatsby....or maybe even Robert Redford. My reverie was disturbed by footsteps behind me. I turned quickly, startled by a sound other than those of the creatures that inhabit the darkness.

"How ya doin'," I said. "Nice night."

"Hey! All right," replied the gentleman in the shadows.

I spent the rest of that evening wondering if the man I had run into in the garden, Robert Redford, daydreamed while at the Boca Raton Resort & Club about actually *being* Jay Gatsby....or maybe even me. ■

Doral

A South Florida swamp, and the man who knew what to do with it

PERHAPS THE MOST FREQUENTLY asked question of the past quarter century has been, What did you know and when did you know it? It apparently has been the most difficult, too, since everyone that has faced it, from dignitaries to designated hitters, has sputtered their way through nearly unintelligible answers while wearing that deer-in-the-headlights look, suffering from, at best, temporary amnesia; at worst, temporary insanity.

But it's a question that appropriately could have been asked of the late Alfred Kaskel before his death in 1968. Consider this: About 30 years ago Kaskel purchased 2,400 acres of swampland, well west of the city of Miami's thriving downtown, at the end of a dirt road without an expressway in sight, nowhere near the beach, and within earshot of one of the busiest international airports in the southern hemisphere. How did he know then that one day the Doral Resort and Country Club would be regarded as one of the premier golf resort destinations in the world?

One reason is that Kaskel appreciated the value of a satisfied customer. A veteran developer and hotelier, Kaskel knew well that if you take care of your guests (and later, of your touring pros and tournament officials), word will get around. And that's exactly what happened—that, and the fact that Doral is *the* place to play in South Florida, and home to one of the most famous golf courses in the country, the Blue Monster.

This Dick Wilson-designed masterpiece is just as it appears on television every March during the Doral Ryder Open: uncompromisingly beautiful, perfectly manicured and very, very long.

Naturally, the distance would be a bit more manageable under less windy conditions, but no matter what time of year you visit, the breeze is always up at Doral, which makes holes on the Blue, like the 591-yard, par-five 12th and the 246-yard, par-three 13th play considerably longer, if that's any consolation.

For sheer excitement, there's nothing like parring the 425-yard, par-four 18th (perennially rated by the pros as one of the most difficult finishing holes on tour). With water on the left from tee to green and that ever-present breeze, however, many a good round has been relegated to the nostalgia heap on this hole.

Not to worry. Doral is much, much more than golf, although with 99 holes (about 19 miles), 100 acres of natural and man-made lakes, and what seems like 1,000 or more bunkers on six great courses, that may be difficult to believe.

Foremost among the amenities is the Doral Saturnia International Spa Resort, a

Below: The 425-yard, par-four 18th of the Blue Monster, rated one of the toughest 'closers' on tour. Right: The Doral Saturnia International Spa Resort.

48-suite, 148,000-square-foot complex designed to get your body in tune with your mind. All spa services—massages, herbal wraps, Swiss showers, loofah scrubs, etc.—are available to the Resort & Country Club guest, and there are Spa Day and Spa Sampler packages designed to fit every schedule and budget. There are also fitness, stress management and image-making workshops, and a spa dining room that serves cuisine based on Saturnia's exclusive Fat-Point™ Nutrition Program.

Saturnia's Mediterranean architecture includes clay-tiled roofs, formal gardens and a 100-foot-long atrium which perfectly complement the Country Club's traditional design.

For the tennis buff there's the 15-court Arthur Ashe Jr. Tennis Center, with eight hard courts (four lighted for night play), seven clay courts and stadium seating for 400.

Transportation to the Doral Ocean Beach Resort (about 20 minutes away) is provided, either for a day at the Aqua Sports Club for scuba instruction, windsurfing or sailing; or for a night at

the renowned Alfredo the Original of Rome restaurant, Miami Beach's most authentic Italian cuisine.

But the most famous amenity at Doral, and the most appreciated, is its incomparable service, a Kaskel legacy. There is no problem too large or too small to be dealt with immediately, and satisfactorily, and the Kaskel family has

DORAL RESORT & COUNTRY CLUB — MIAMI, FLORIDA

LOCATION: 4400 Northwest 87 Avenue, Miami, FL 33178; seven miles west of Miami International Airport.

ACCOMMODATIONS: 650 rooms and suites; 48 suites at the Saturnia International Spa Resort.

DINING/ENTERTAINMENT: Provare Italian Restaurant, classic cuisine, extensive wine list; Sandpiper Steak & Seafood Restaurant; Champions Restaurant & Bar; The Staggerbush Bar and Lawn Grill; Rousseau's Lounge; Water Hazard Bar & Grill.

AMENITIES: 99 holes of golf; 15-court tennis complex; swimming pool open 24 hours; fishing; cycling; game room. Spa facilities available for guest use.

MEETING FACILITIES: 75,000 square feet of function space; Grand Ballroom accommodates up to 1,000.

RATES: From $225 to $630.

RESERVATIONS: Call (800) 22-DORAL.

maintained and enhanced the tradition of excellence begun by its founder.

Although the tournament has since its inception offered the pros one of the largest purses on tour (that makes them *very* happy), the most telling anecdote from Doral involved a PGA tournament official who, during one of the CBS-televised events, suggested that a bridge between the ninth green and 10th tee would be more convenient, believing that Kaskel would get around to it....someday.

At the end of play that day, however, Kaskel rounded up a crew, worked through the night and had the bridge ready before the first group teed off. "It was a good idea," Kaskel said, "and I didn't see any reason why we should wait to make things better."

Making things better is commonplace at Doral. The property seems to be in a constant state of upgrading, as if perfection could be improved upon.

The Red Course, for example, has in the past few years been modestly redesigned, and the director of golf operations envisions it becoming "the second championship-caliber course at Doral." Though there's absolutely no chance it will ever supplant the Blue Monster, no one is rushing to bet against his assessment. They've seen what is possible at Doral, and that's just about anything.

Superior golf, luxurious, centrally located accommodations, an amenities package that ranks among the best, and a family's commitment to excellence, all standard operating procedure at Doral.

What did Alfred Kaskel know? Obviously a lot more than the rest of us.

And when did he know it? A lot sooner than anyone else. ■

Harbour Ridge

Two of the finest Florida courses you may never play

TO BE HONEST, I'VE NEVER SPENT the night at Harbour Ridge. I've never had dinner there, frolicked in the pool, played tennis or docked in the marina. This report doesn't address boating, fishing, cycling or jogging. Rumor has it that the 885-acre development will soon cancel its resort offerings—40 furnished garden apartments used as rental units—and by the time you read this perhaps the only way you'll be able to play the golf courses at Harbour Ridge is to purchase property there, if there is any left to purchase.

Harbour Ridge, on the banks of the mile-wide St. Lucie River just north of Stuart, opened its first golf course in 1984 to rave reviews, and Golden Marsh was among the six Florida courses included on a 1987 list of the 65 "best courses built after 1965" by members of the American Society of Golf Course Architects, the National Golf Foundation and the Golf Course Superintendents of America. High praise indeed for such a relatively young layout.

This Joe Lee design plays to 6,607

yards, and is imposing without being brutish, although water comes into play on 14 holes, marsh is in play on four others, and 11 holes dogleg either left or right.

Still, the longest par-four is but 408 yards and the par-fives top-out at 524 yards, with one a mere 488. That's not to say that Lee has crafted a pushover here. Far from it. Golf writer James Fitchette says that the bunkering at Golden Marsh "indicates the line of play as much as punish errant shots." That's easy for him to say, and it's only true when you're playing your approach shots from alongside the bunkers rather than *from* them.

Pete and P.B. Dye's River Ridge course, on the other hand, has been described as a "basher's course." Whereas Golden Marsh can be a driver/8-iron course under perfect conditions—and from the forward tees—River Ridge, at 6,626 yards (only 17 yards longer than Golden Marsh), is more like driver/8-iron...8-iron, even on the best of days. The 470-yard par-4 eighth hole, for instance, absolutely requires a fairway wood to a green that more resembles a pool table than a putting surface.

But nothing compares to the iron-pumping exercise provided by a four-hole stretch on the outward nine, Nos. 3, 4, 5 and 6. No. 3 is a 425-yard, par-four dogleg left that features water running the length of the fairway on the right side and a putting surface well bunkered on the left. No. 4 follows with 418 yards of dogleg right with an approach over the marsh to a green virtually surrounded by sand.

River Ridge then stacks back-to-back par-fives—the 527-yard fifth and the 515-yard sixth—both of which offer one *or more* shots over water. There is no "going out in 33" here. River Ridge will test you at every turn. You can never let down and simply hope to post a good number, not with the Dye-signature undulating fairways, pot bunkers that require steps for entry and exit and greens that are, in Fitchette's words, "roller-coaster putting surfaces."

There is one other thing about Harbour Ridge that you ought to know: The developers (chairman John Dodge and president Jack Schuler) are firmly committed to protecting the environment. When bald eagle nesting sites were discovered on the property, the golf courses were re-routed and a 26-acre sanctuary was imposed around the nest. All digging in the area was done by hand so as not to disturb the eaglets. For this and many other commendable reasons the Florida Audobon Society in 1988 bestowed upon Harbour Ridge its Corporate Award "for outstanding service to the environment."

Which is further evidence that although eagles are readily found on the golf courses at Harbour Ridge, birdies are much more difficult to come by.

You may have to take my word on this. Unfortunately, you may never have the opportunity to play these two outstanding courses. But if you were to call (407) 336-1800, and tell them you're interested in seeing and possibly purchasing property, who knows? You'll either receive an invitation to visit, or you'll be politely referred to the nature trail, and told to take a walk. ■

The Inverrary

Ft. Lauderdale's return to the good old days

I KNOW WHAT YOU'RE THINKING: "I'd rather light my hair on fire than vacation in Ft. Lauderdale, where hordes of incorrigible post-pubescents have turned intelligent life as we know it into a never-ending, mind-numbing light beer commercial, in which nubile young women and taut young men frolic in the surf, play beach volleyball and para-sail, incredibly at the SAME TIME.

It really isn't like that. Since local authorities put a loosely tightened lid on such frivolity in the mid-1980s, Ft. Lauderdale has, in a way, returned to its fashionably elegant former self. That's not to say that fun (a lot of fun) is a thing of the past. It's now simply a bit more refined, a bit more debonair.

A perfect example is The Inverrary Resort, a former conference center that happened to have access to an outstanding golf club. Remember the Jackie Gleason—then the American Motors, then the Honda—Inverrary Classic? Remember when the Tournament Players Championship rotated from course to course and the third TPC, in 1976, was played at Inverrary? That's *this* Inverrary.

Club Corporation acquired the property in the late '80s, then renovated and reopened it in 1988 with a sharper focus on the resort side of the operation. Amenities were enhanced and added, rooms were made more luxurious and an air of casual elegance began to blow again in Ft. Lauderdale.

That "air" had a few golf balls in it, too. It's been that way since Robert Trent Jones and his son Rees designed the East and West courses at Inverrary as championship-caliber layouts capable of hosting PGA Tour (and LPGA Tour) events.

The West is the more poular course for the true resort golfer. At only 6,621 yards from the championship tees (5,930 from the middle), good, solid strategic golf will net you a good score. If you play with a ball that floats, that is. Water is an obstacle on 12 holes, never more so deviously than on the 447-yard, par-four 10th—which obviously requires a good bash off the

tee—that doglegs slightly left and has water tee-to-green on that same side. But this is the exception rather than the rule. There are a sufficient number of sub-400 yard par-fours to make you feel pretty good about yourself.

The par-threes are a different story, however. The shortest—at 179 yards—is No. 3. The longest—at 197 yards—is the cross-the-water-twice No. 8, a nail biter when the wind is up or when you're playing in the rain.

The East course is a whomping, stomping 7,124 yards and carries a course rating of 74.8; you'd better to be ready to fly out of your Foot-Joys on this big dog. And golf holes like the 215-yard, par-3 sixth and the 580-yard, par-5 eighth make better-than-average fairway-wood play essential. (Hit it far and straight here, though, and you can really be somebody.)

The facility is rounded out by a par-61 executive course, which is a pleasant warmup for the East or West, or a relaxing way to spend a late afternoon.

Inverrary also comprises 30 tennis courts at the Racquet Club, three swimming pools and an exercise facility where you can work off the previous evening's dinner at the Oak Room, the resort's elegant, intimate restaurant that features fresh local seafood and a remarkable wine selection.

For nightlife there's the Long Green Lounge at the resort or the myriad of clubs and lounges in the Ft. Lauderdale area. In that same region can be found jai-alai, horseracing, greyhound racing, canal cruising or even rodeo.

If you're looking for excitement, we suggest you try one of the aforementioned activities and leave the boogie-boarding to the kids. Not that you couldn't boogie board if you *wanted* to, but it does play hell with your Armani loafers. ■

THE INVERRARY RESORT — FT. LAUDERDALE, FLA.

LOCATION: 3501 Inverrary Blvd., Ft. Lauderdale, FL 33319; 20 minutes northwest of Ft. Lauderdale International Airport.

ACCOMMODATIONS: 198 guest rooms including four suites; private balconies.

DINING/ENTERTAINMENT: The Cypress Terrace, casual breakfast, lunch and dinner overlooking the pool; The Oak Room, elegant gourmet dining; Long Green Lounge, nightly entertainment and happy hour.

AMENITIES: 36 holes of golf; 18-hole executive course; three swimming pools; fully equipped exercise facility with aerobics; 30 tennis courts (eight lighted); croquet; jogging course.

MEETING FACILITIES: 14,000 square feet of flexible space for groups of 10 to 700.

RATES: Hotel currently closed for renovation.

RESERVATIONS: Call (800) 327-8661.

Lely Resort

Trent Jones strikes again, this time in the "Florida Rockies"

WHEN IS A RESORT NOT REALLY A resort at all? When it's Lely Resort, a 2,800-acre residential community in Naples that is the site of (in my opinion) one of Florida's top three public golf courses. Lely may become a true resort in the near future, or the distant future, or perhaps never. A hotel has been on the drawing board for some time, but ground has not yet been broken and for now it seems to have taken a back seat on the priority bus.

The Classics, an 18-hole course designed by Gary Player, has recently begun operations, but it is a members-only course for residents of the community which doesn't allow outside play.

Which is fine, considering the open-to-the-public Flamingo Island Club is a 7,171-yard Robert Trent Jones masterpiece with severely undulating fairways, water in play on 12 holes and man-made features unlike any other in the state. "When we started, this was probably the flattest land anyone ever created, including God," says Trent Jones. "Now it's a beautiful piece of rugged terrain with rolling turf and lots of water."

Trent Jones obviously knows what he's talking about, having designed more than 450 golf courses over the past 60 years, and being one of only two course architects inducted into the World Golf Hall of Fame.

What he has constructed at Lely is a paralyzingly beautiful layout with all par-four holes exceeding 390 yards, par-threes that begin at 184 yards and run to 213, and a few marathon-like par-fives, including the 567-yard third hole and the 596-yard seventh—not surprisingly the No. 1 handicap hole on the course.

But par-fives of this ilk are guaranteed three-shot holes, anyway; it's the par-fours that can hurt you at Flamingo Island, the 422-yard eighth, for example. No. 8 is a tight dogleg left that plays down a tree-lined fairway to a 70-degree turn, over water, into a very, very small putting surface. Sand bunkers of considerable depth and breadth protect the bail-out areas in the fairway and around the green, and birdie here is usually not an option. Bogey, yes; birdie, no.

Likewise on the 422-yard 16th, which on the card looks straightaway but must be played with a drawing tee shot, a fading approach and frequently some hair-raising sand work to close it out. Putting is never a problem here: The greens, while undulating, aren't nearly as twisting and turning as the fairways.

There are a few oh-by-the-way holes, such as the 405-yard first and the 426-yard 10th, but I'd like to think that Trent Jones gave us these as a gift, really, to get us out of the box on the front and back with our wits still about us. No. 1 does have water protecting the green on the left side, and with fairway bunkers protecting the right you're required to fade your second shot over the lagoon into the green. But No. 10 is all in front of you, straight down the middle with your drive, a healthy 6-iron or muscular seven and you're putting for a three. Make it here if you can; your chances diminish condsiderably the closer you get to the clubhouse.

You'll notice I have yet to mention the par-threes. There's good reason for that: I'm trying my best to forget them, at least for now. I hit 5-wood into a stiff breeze on the 204-yard second and two-putted for par. I hit 4-iron to the 184-yard sixth and two-putted that. Then I splashed a 3-iron on the 204-yard 12th, twice, for a seven, and dunked a 2-iron, twice, on the 213-yard 14th—Flamingo Island Club's signature hole—for an eight. You can't make a very good number when you go nine over par on two holes on the same side of a golf course, can you?

Scoring well, however, isn't as important as playing well (I read that once), and playing well isn't nearly as important as enjoying yourself on the course. (Both these little ditties were no doubt penned by a 36-handicapper.) I must tell you that although I failed to set the course record—the upper end of it, at least—I thoroughly enjoyed the layout, about which one player said, "It's like playing golf in the Florida Rockies." Obviously that's a gross overstatement, but Trent Jones moved enough dirt into enough un-Florida-like positions to make you think you're somewhere else. And somewhere else, when it comes to the Flamingo Island Club at Lely Resort, is no place I want to be. ■

For information call (813) 793-2223.

Marriott's Marco Island Resort

THERE ARE A SELECT FEW PLACES where the turquoise waters of the Gulf of Mexico actually out-Bahama the Bahamas—where the water is so sparklingly clear that you can see the bottom from 100 feet or more. One of those places is Marco Island, a slice of tropical paradise off Florida's southernmost Gulf Coast and the site of the region's largest resort, Marriott's Marco Island Resort & Golf Club. It's also the site of "one of America's best new golf courses," according to *Golf Digest*, a 6,925-yard Joe Lee design carved from the mangroves and forests of Australian pine and palm that are indigenous to the area.

The Golf Club at Marco weaves its way through intricate waterways and dew-soaked bogs, and water is in full play on 15 holes. Exceptionally wide fairway landing areas, however, offer the golfer an opportunity to score well, though early. Matching par on the outward nine is feasible. Limping home on the inward nine is probable.

The longest hole on the course is the 547-yard, par-5 ninth, a sharp dogleg right with a reservoir bordering the turn into the severely sloped putting surface. Fading the ball is perilous, but no more so than a draw, which requires starting the ball out over the reservoir and *wishing* it back toward center, hoping meanwhile that the northeast winds which frequently cross the course don't escort your ball to an early exit. It's a great way to make the turn onto the more wet, more exacting back half.

No. 11 is another par-five (of only 519 yards, however) that doglegs to the right and has water right and heavy bunkering left. Unlike the ninth, the 11th is reachable in two, if you are capable of carrying a channel of water protecting the extremely narrow green in front. This green is much more receptive to a pitching wedge than a 3-wood, and I believe it's usually *(always)* preferable playing your third shot on a par-five from 100 yards in front of the green rather than 10 yards off the back. You can easily make four here; you can just as easily make eight.

The signature 16th hole is a 165-yard par-three that plays from a bulkheaded tee to a bulkheaded green surrounded by deep bunkering and sand. I've hit everything from 3-iron to 8-iron here—depending on the wind—and have failed to make birdie in any attempt, though I once holed a tee shot. Unfortunately it was my second tee shot, the first having found its way to the bottom of the surrounding lake. Oh well.

Accommodations at Marco Island are in the form of 735 luxurious rooms, suites, villas and lanais with private balconies overlooking the Gulf or the lush island interior. The lobby of the hotel is accented by cream-colored marble floors and coquina rock pillars and is surrounded by a 15-acre garden of coconut, Chinese fan and sabal palms. In fact, more than 15,000 annuals dot the facility with vivid splashes of red, yellow and pink.

Miles of white-sand beach border the hotel and golf course, and shelling at Marriott's Marco Island Resort, as in the entire surrounding area, yields lightning welks, horse conchs, sharks' eyes, calico scallops and lion's paws. And more than a few Titleists. ■

MARRIOTT'S MARCO ISLAND RESORT

LOCATION: 400 South Collier Blvd., Marco Island, FL 33937; 15 miles south of Naples.

ACCOMMODATIONS: 735 rooms and suites.

DINING/ENTERTAINMENT: Marco Dining Room & Grille, Continental cuisine, dinner only; The Voyager, casual dining, fresh seafood overlooking the Gulf; Cafe del Sol, family atmosphere; Quinn's on the Beach, casual all-day dining, live entertainment nightly; Caxambus Lounge, entertainment and dancing; Tiki Bar & Grill, lunch, snacks, beverages.

AMENITIES: 18 holes of golf; lighted tennis; three swimming pools; health club; offshore and backwater fishing; jogging course.

MEETING FACILITIES: 48,000 square feet including 19,000-square-foot Grand Ballroom.

RATES: From approx. $90 to $150 per night.

RESERVATIONS: Call (813) 394-2511.

Palm Beach Polo & Country Club

POLO AND GOLF HAVE A LOT MORE in common than most people imagine. Both games are played with sticks and balls, both (unfortunately, if you're a walking golfer) employ a "vehicle" to take the player from one shot to the next, both utilize a great deal of open space (polo fields are 10 times the size of football fields) and both seem to *require* apparel that borders on the garish.

At Palm Beach Polo & Country Club, however, the affinity between the two runs much deeper. Recognized as the international headquarters for the sport of polo, PBPCC had to "build up" its golf facilities to match the golf courses many of the club's members were used to playing—clubs like Winged Foot, Shinnecock Hills, Butler National and Oakmont.

To compete with the horsey set, Landmark Land (which purchased the property in 1986) brought in their favorite designer, Pete Dye, who by 1988 had completed 12 courses (among them the infamous Stadium Course at PGA West) for Landmark.

Along with son P.B., Dye designed and constructed a 7,116-yard monster of a course, Cypress, which features six par-fours of 420 yards or longer, the key phrase being "or longer." No. 13, for example, plays an overbearing 462 yards, has water tee-to-green on the right side and water virtually surrounding the green. And the closing hole, the 450-yard, par-four 18th, has water down the entire left side and a putting surface stuck back in the left-hand corner of the right-side playing fairway.

But there's no match (in all of golf, practically) for the incredibly long, incredibly difficult 641-yard, par-five 17th. Stop and think about 641 yards for a moment. That's two aircraft carriers in a rear-end collision. Or 8,000 rolls of dimes in a row. Or about three times further than my normal tee shot. On it I suffered the ultimate golfing indignity: going 10 over par on a single hole.

This is the same hole where, if memory serves, Arnold Palmer once made a 13. "How did you make a 13 out there, Arnie?" asked a member of the media later in the clubhouse. "I missed the putt for 12," replied the scowling Palmer.

Still, if played from the forward tees (I simply *must* begin teeing it there) the Cypress Course at 6,039 yards is eminently do-able, even though the first hole is the last one you'll see without water in play. From the forward tees you can hit 3-woods on all of the par-fours, and the two most difficult par-threes—No. 6 at 197 yards, and No. 16 at 231 yards—shrink to 150 and 143 yards, respectively. And from those forward tees that notorious No. 17 is scaled down to a benign 520 yards, which seems to be only about half as long as it is from the back.

In fact, the difference from member tees to championship tees is probably 10 strokes or better. Decide that morning how well you can live with yourself if you shoot in the 80s, 90s or low 100s, then drop your ball in the appropriate spot and let it rip.

The Ron Garl/Jerry Pate-designed Dunes Course, only 66 yards shorter than Cypress, nevertheless plays somewhat "easier." Only three par-fours exceed my 420-yard limit for brutishness, and the par-threes run between 180 and 230 yards. The par-fives, though, begin at 520 yards and move upward to 550, and the only holes where you can't get your ball wet are the ninth and the 17th.

Still, holes like the 331-yard, par-4 second and the 374-yard 14th offer a chance to post a decent overall score, and the Dunes (completed in 1984) will soothe you with its Scottish-links feel—extensive mounding, pot bunkering, and undulating fairways—that comes to you without benefit of howling winds and sub-freezing temperatures.

The Tom and George Fazio executive course is a perfect complement to the fine golf facilities at Palm Beach Polo & Country Club. On it you can hone your short game and practice your medium to long irons, and also fine-tune your wardrobe. I'm not that crazy about current polo *or* golf attire, but I've seen a sport on TV whose players wear outfits I could really get behind. I think it's called professional wrestling. ■

PALM BEACH POLO & COUNTRY CLUB — WEST PALM BEACH, FLA.

LOCATION: 13198 Forest Hill Blvd., West Palm Beach FL 33414.

ACCOMMODATIONS: Studio, one-, two- and three-bedroom residences, located adjacent to or near the sporting complexes.

DINING/ENTERTAINMENT: Private club facilities including five dining rooms located in the three clubhouses on property. Casual and formal dining is available in a variety of atmospheres.

AMENITIES: 45 holes of golf (Ron Garl/Jerry Pate, Pete Dye/P.B. Dye; nine-hole executive course by Tom and George Fazio); 24-court tennis complex; full equestrian facilities including grand prix ring, four show rings, schooling area and two barns; 10 polo fields and two practice fields; swimming; fitness center; croquet.

RATES: Call for rates.

RESERVATIONS: Call (407) 798-7000.

PGA National Resort & Spa

Don't worry, it's the same old 'National' . . . only better

AS ONE WHO WAS SEEMINGLY "SET in his ways" at birth, I find myself increasingly disturbed by change, especially since it so infrequently is for the better, and especially since it so often affects the things I've come to know and love. Oh, I weathered the Edsel and the Nehru jacket okay, but I was crestfallen when I was forced to trade my wide-mouthed glass mustard jar for a "new and improved" squeezeable plastic container, one that leaves fully one-third of the product stuck to the narrow sides and bottom of the package, forcing me to either cut into it with garden shears (and nearly lose a digit in the process) or to just throw it away, with all the attendant waste. (This is *improved?*) And I actually wept over the Coke/New Coke/Classic Coke debacle.

So it was with some trepidation that I visited PGA National Resort & Spa recently—for the first time. You see, the first few times I was a guest at the resort it was called, simply, PGA National. That always seemed to be enough. The resort is the home of the PGA of America (headquartered there since 1976) and the U.S. Croquet Association. It also comprises five outstanding 18-hole golf courses (one of which, The Champion, hosts a Senior PGA Tour *major*), and its hotel contains 335 recently refurbished guest rooms and suites. All of which led me to believe that the property and its moniker sufficed as is, or was.

When it was announced in 1991 that a European-style spa would be opening in early '92, and that the resort would hence be called PGA National Resort & Spa, for some reason I envisioned the fairways at the resort crowded with men and women in mud packs and body wraps, not playing the game for the thrill of it or the fun of it or the tradition of it, but simply using the golf courses—my golf courses—to kill the time between their Shiatsu massage and a salt-glo loofah scrub.

Don't ask me why I thought this. I know it didn't happen at Doral or Bonaventure or even Palm-Aire, but for the first few months after the initial announcement, the "itch" that change has caused in the past was once again proving to be unscratchable.

Thankfully, and not surprisingly, this scenario is not what has transpired. PGA National remains one of the premier golf destinations in the U.S., and just so happens to contain a delightful spa that lives up to its pre-opening PR: "...to enhance PGA National's renowned facilities for a complete sports, spa and resort experience."

First, though, the golf. PGA National's five courses are an eclectic mix from some of the bonafide geniuses in golf architecture. The Haig, The Squire and The Champion courses were designed by the late George Fazio and his nephew Tom and opened in 1981 (Champion was subsequently redesigned by Jack Nicklaus in 1990). The Estate course—the National's most recent addition—was designed by Karl Litten, and The General was designed by and named for the only professional golfer to ever enlist an *army* of supporters, Arnold Palmer.

Trying to pick a personal favorite from this delighful assortment would be difficult were it not for the fact that one has humbled me—humiliated me, time and time again—which of course automatically makes it my favorite: The Champion. This 7,022-yard beauty has repeatedly brought me to my knees, my most enthusiastic genuflection occurring on that

With water in play on seemingly every hole, golf at PGA National requires sound course management.

recent visit when I went an astounding 12-over-par (that's not a misprint) after four holes. Oddly, I finished the round 14-over, so the course is playable from the tips, even for a 12- to 14-handicapper like me. But getting out of the box strong is necessary on The Champion; you need to be stepping onto the fourth tee at even par or one-over if you wish to card a good score.

The problem is the first three holes offer nothing but trouble on the left side, and if your ball moves right-to-left, well, you can see the difficulty. No. 1 is practically straightaway, a 362-yard par four, and a good poke from the elevated tees should put you in position for an 8- or 9-iron approach. I find myself usually playing that approach from the left rough, as trees and a sand bunker pretty much fill up (in my mind's eye, anyway) the right side. If the rough is heavy, as it was on that record-setting day of mine, it can twist your club in your hands, sending your snap-hooked second shot to a watery grave *(double bogey).*

Ditto for No. 2, a 434-yard par-four dogleg-left which requires something

along the lines of a 3-iron to get home. Another snap-hook later (into the water), and then one into the sand and another left there, and I was well on my way *(triple bogey).*

No. 3 is a straightaway par-five of 539 yards and, yes, I hooked my second shot into the water *(triple bogey).* By the time I reached the 375-yard, par-4 fourth my clubs were acting like divining rods,

PGA NATIONAL RESORT & SPA — PALM BEACH GARDENS, FLA.

LOCATION: 400 Avenue Of The Champions, Palm Beach Gardens, FL 33418; 15 miles north of Palm Beach International Airport.

ACCOMMODATIONS: 335 guest rooms including 57 suites and 85 cottage suites.

DINING/ENTERTAINMENT: Explorers, formal gourmet dining; Colonel Bogey's, casual brunch and dinner; The Citrus Tree, indoor-outdoor cafe; Breakaway Sports Pub & Eatery; Health Bar; 19th Hole; Legends Lounge.

AMENITIES: 90 holes of golf; 19 tennis courts; three swimming pools; Health & Racquet Club; European-style spa; 26-acre sailing lake; croquet; youth program; Nicklaus/Flick Golf School; The Academy of Golf.

MEETING FACILITIES: 30,000 square feet; PGA Grand Ballroom accommodates 850.

RATES: From $95 to $900.

RESERVATIONS: Call (800) 633-9150.

Above: PGA National's main pool and a portion of its 26-acre lake. Right: Nicklaus' redesign of The Champion included the 431-yard, par-four 12th.

searching out the wet stuff and doing whatever it took to get my ball there. Indeed, the fourth hole is one of only two on Champion where water actually is *not* in play (the other is the par-five 10th), although there is a lagoon adjacent to the tee which under normal circumstances would be impossible to find, even with Lewis and Clark blazing the trail. It took an extraordinary effort to shank my drive a perfect 90 degrees from the tee box to accomplish the feat *(quadruple bogey)*. But hey! That's golf.

The Squire and The Haig, named in honor of Gene Sarazen and Walter Hagen, respectively, offer somewhat of a respite, in distance anyway. Water abounds on these courses as well: It comes into play on all 18 on Squire and on 15 of the 18 on Haig.

At 6,478 yards, Squire requires sound course management—knowing when to leave the driver in the bag in favor of a 3- or 4-wood is imperative here. The 6,806-yard Haig, however, allows you to step onto the tee, especially on holes such as the 566-yard, par-5 fourth and the 456-yard, par-four 18th, and whale away.

The General, too, has water nearly everywhere you could think to place it and, except for the 541-yard, par-5 eighth, the 429-yard, par-four 17th and the 567-yard, par-five 18th, your best bet is to rely on your mid- to long-irons and let your short game (You do have a short game, don't you?) take up the slack.

The Estate course, alas, is currently an unknown for me, although at 6,327 yards, with a slope of 131 and water on 13 holes, I expect no more and no less than I receive from the other four.

About the spa: No, it doesn't have its own accommodations; nor is it on the scale of, say, Doral Saturnia. But, yes, it does offer the facilities, the programs and—most importantly—the service of the finest spas in Florida, and 17 of the hotel rooms that lead to the courtyard surrounding the spa have been redecorated and dedicated to spa-going guests. The motif is a variation (tiled floors and vaulted ceilings) of the Mediterranean Revival theme of the rest of the hotel, and the requisite spa menu is served in three of the restaurants on the property.

For formal dining, however, Explorers offers Continental cuisine in an elegant, very private atmosphere. The extensive wine list and the impeccable service in Explorers make it a must for every guest. Colonel Bogey's offers casual dining for dinner and a delectable Sunday brunch, while The Citrus Tree is a poolside indoor/outdoor cafe serving breakfast and lunch.

These amenities, along with the truly excellent golf facilities, including the PGA Academy of Golf and the Nicklaus/Flick Golf School, have made PGA National somewhat of a legend in only 12 short years. The resort has been the recipient of the Mobil Four-Star and AAA Four-Diamond ratings for eight years in a row, along with numerous other awards from national publications for tennis, golf and meeting facilities. It also has hosted the PGA Championship (1987) and the Ryder Cup matches (1983), and annually hosts the PGA Senior's Championship.

In addition, PGA National is the only East Coast site of THEclinic, offering the acclaimed Egoscue Method of physical training, athletic performance enhancement and rehabilitation (one of the reasons Jack Nicklaus still plays the game).

All of which goes to show that change actually can be for the better. Now that they've been sucessful at PGA National, however, maybe we can get back to work on that mustard jar. ■

The Breakers

Painstakingly posh Palm Beach panache

I DON'T HAVE A PROBLEM WITH IT. A few die-hard golfers reject the notion that The Breakers in Palm Beach, Fla., is a true "golf" resort because the resort's Ocean Course (on the property) is short (5,956 yards), moderately bunkered and without an abundance of water hazards, especially considering its South Florida location. That doesn't bother me. Never has. I've never been able to match par there (70), and oddly, neither have the whiners I've known who have belittled the facility as *too easy.* Hey! When you start shooting 62s, regularly, come see me. Otherwise, lighten up.

Of course, with the 1968 addition of Breakers West—25 minutes from the hotel in West Palm Beach—you can find all the length (7,101 yards) and all the water (in play on 13 holes) you've been clamoring for. And while I heartily recommend you play the Breakers West course during your visit, you're doing yourself a disservice by rejecting the resort course out-of-hand—if anyone would even consider rejecting a course originally built by the legendary Donald Ross at the turn of the century.

And even if the Ocean Course were a par-27 pitch-and-putt, the accommodations, amenities and service at The Breakers make it a "must see" in South Florida; a "must do," actually, since the activities at the resort and in the surrounding Palm Beach area will keep you busy much longer than from sun up to sunset.

This is a resort of the first order, designed by Leonard Schultze of Waldorf-Astoria fame in 1926 and listed on the National Register of Historic Places. The

The Ocean Course requires exacting golf shots through dense stands of Florida palms and pines.

hotel of today is actually the third built on the property (the first two were destroyed by fire), and its current 600,000 square feet of space set on 140 acres of beachfront—as close as you can get to the Gulf Stream and still be on *terra firma*—was reached in 1969 with the construction of two additional wings. Along the way there have been numerous upgrades and renovations, and the resort is currently involved in a five-year, $50 million refurbishment.

The Breakers Ocean Course is the site each year of the Palm Beach Golf Classic, which in the past has featured PGA Tour stars such as Sam Snead, Jack Nicklaus (who once shot a sub-60 round there), Ben Crenshaw and Raymond Floyd. In my estimation it is a "perfect" resort course, obviously not overbearingly long (no par-fours longer than 400 yards) nor overwhelmingly wet (you could die of thirst before you're able to find water here).

The lone par-three on the outward nine is a mere 125 yards, and a "fading" 125 at that. There are no par-fives on the front side, and the single par-five on the back (No. 14, at 460 yards) would be a lock for birdie were it not for a lone, oversized sand bunker in the exact center of the landing area. Finesse your drive left of the bunker, or crush it (your choice), and eagle is not out of the question. Kick one around in that bunker and you could be here awhile.

The two par-threes on the back play in excess of 200 yards: No. 10 says 200 on the scorecard, but the prevailing breezes from the Gulf Stream make it somewhat longer; No. 13, at 225 yards, has been known to demand your big-

THE BREAKERS
Palm Beach, Florida

LOCATION: 1 South County Road, Palm Beach, FL 33480; approximately four miles from Palm Beach International Airport.

ACCOMMODATIONS: 526 guest rooms, 36 suites, two Presidential suites and two Imperial suites.

DINING/ENTERTAINMENT: The Florentine Room, fine dining, exceptional wine list, orchestra; Beach Club, casual indoor dining with views of the ocean and pool, Sunday brunch; Beach Club Patio, casual al fresco dining for lunch daily; Fairways Cafe, breakfast, lunch and snacks overlooking the Ocean Golf Club; Circle Dining Room, breakfast a la carte and buffet; Alcazar Lounge, afternoon tea, cocktail service and nightly entertainment.

AMENITIES: 36 holes of golf (Donald Ross, William Byrd); 20 tennis courts, 11 lighted for night play; private beach; swimming pool and wading pool; fitness center with sauna, steam rooms, massage, Nautilus equipment and free weights; all water sports including snorkeling, scuba diving and sailing; croquet; supervised children's program; shops and boutiques.

MEETING FACILITIES: More than 36,000 square feet of space, including the versatile Mediterranean and Venetian Ballrooms; comprehensive business center; full-service audio/visual department.

RATES: Rooms from $125 to $470; suites from $350 to $1,800.

RESERVATIONS: Call (800) 833-3141 or (407) 655-6611.

gest club on exceptionally windy days (upwind, that is). When the wind swirls, as it often does, or is at your back you can get there with a 7-iron.

Breakers West, on the other hand, has only one par-four that doesn't reach 400 yards, and it's close at 396. The par-threes begin at 180 yards (No. 8) and top out at 225 yards (No. 17). The only par-five on the front side of this par-71 course (No. 6) is an emminently reachable 530 yards, but has water running its entire length down the right side and cutting into the fairway at approximately the same position as a lay-up 5-iron or a muffed 3-wood.

The back nine, at nearly 3,650 yards, features the lone sub-400-yard par-four, the 13th, with water tee to green down the left and almost completely surrounding the putting surface. By the way, the bail out area for the tee shot has two large bunkers collecting a toll from the reckless.

The awesome 600-yard, par-five 14th follows immediately thereafter. Obviously this is a three-shot hole (3-wood, 4-wood, 8- or 9-iron is not inappropriate here), and the secret to scoring well on this hole is to keep the ball on the right side tee to green, even though that's the side with the water hazard. Patience is prerequisite on both courses; perhaps more so on Breakers West, where the urge is to bite off as much of the 7,000-plus yards as you think you can chew.

Other amenities at The Breakers include 20 tennis courts, a private strand of beach, a competition-size swimming pool, a fitness center with Nautilus equipment, free weights and aerobics, snorkeling, scuba diving, sailing, etc., etc. A highlight is the shopping arcade with a multitude of outstanding individual boutiques offering the finest in men's and women's wear, jewelry and gems and golf and tennis apparel. The shops, as well as the rest of The Breakers amenities and services, are manned, well, *peopled*, by a staff of over 1,200 who speak a total of 17 languages (you'll always be able to *communicate* at The Breakers).

Area attractions include the Greater Palm Beach Symphony, the Jai Alai Fronton and shopping on world-famous Worth Avenue.

Dining is an "experience" at The Breakers, especially in the Florentine Room, which features the finest in American and Continental cuisine and a wine list with over 500 vintages. A personal favorite is the Sunday brunch at the Beach Club, a three-hour extravaganza of food, fun and fashion (as in what the other guests are wearing).

So, considering the activities, the amenities and the fine dining, perhaps The Breakers isn't a true "golf" resort after all. But it will certainly *do*, as it has for the past 65 years, until something better comes along. ■

Turnberry Isle Yacht & Country Club

THERE ARE A FEW THINGS THAT I look for when I check into an upscale golf resort, like teak wood, silk and imported marble decorating the inside of my room, three telephones with two lines each (you can buy *and* sell at the same time), remote-control television with VCR (with a mini TV in the bath), honor bar, in-room whirlpool and separate shower, bathrobes, toiletries and fresh-cut flowers. (I think that about covers it.) Those luxuries also happen to be standard at Turnberry Isle Yacht & Country Club in Aventura, a member of The Leading Hotels of the World and a Mobil Four-Star Award winner for many of the 20 years since developer Don Soffer first unlocked the doors.

In mid-1988 Rafael Hotels Ltd. became half owner and full manager of the resort, and the first thing they did was pump, oh, *$80 million* into the property. As you would expect, $80 million goes a very long way; it went far enough at Turnberry to transform it from a merely great resort to a fantastic one.

Among the new additions at Turnberry is the Country Club complex, which includes a 271-room hotel of luxury rooms and suites, two Robert Trent Jones golf courses (from the old days), restaurants and lounges, 16 tennis courts and their respective pro shops. The lobby is complemented with marble, as is most of the resort, and pillars, arches and red-tile roofs lend a Mediterranean flavor (with Addison Mizner mixed in) to the surroundings. The hotel rooms are bedecked in the requisite marble, terra-cotta tile floors, ceiling fans and blonde-wood furniture, and "elegant" and "luxurious" are the two words that first come to mind.

There's also the Marina Hotel with 55 rooms and suites, some as large as 1,600 square feet—all with views of the Intracoastal Waterway and the Turnberry Marina—and the exclusive Yacht Club Hotel with just 14 rooms and suites. Boat owners can dock at the marina in one of 117 slips (for yachts up to 150 feet) and enjoy all the privileges of hotel guests.

The Spa at Turnberry is filled with Nautilus and Cybex equipment, free weights, racquetball courts, Lifecycles, treadmills and rowing machines, and offers all levels of aerobic exercise. On staff at the spa is a doctor, nutritionist, Nautilus trainers, fitness instructors and massage therapists. Spa services run the gamut from salt-glow loofa treatments, herbal body wraps, facials, nutritional counseling and personalized spa menus.

Now that you've been pampered at

the spa, it's time to take your medicine on the golf courses.

The North Course (par-70) is by far the shortest of the two at only 6,323 yards, but tight doglegs and well-protected greens are the order of the day here, and a few holes (the 562-yard, par-5 fifth comes immediately to mind) will humble you if you're not thinking clearly. No. 5 doesn't really dogleg right, it sort of meanders in that direction until you're within 100 yards or so of the green. Then it turns a sharp 90 degrees into the putting surface, with water running down the right side and heavy bunkering to the left. A mammoth drive will leave you with the impression that it's a two-shot hole. It isn't. Play safe and you might, just might, make birdie. Probably not.

The par-72 South Course is a mind-bending 7,0003 yards; I thought on the day I played it that my 3-wood had been surgically attached to my hands. And with two par-threes over 200 yards long, much of the day is spent in the "grip it and rip it" mode.

Still, "bash" golf is a game I enjoy, though admittedly one I don't play that well. The day I played the South Course I reached out and touched someone using both lines of my three telephones, calling my club pro at home for advice...and my therapist for solace. ■

TURNBERRY ISLE - AVENTURA, FLORIDA

LOCATION: 19999 West Country Club Dr., Aventura, FL 33180; 15 minutes south of Ft. Lauderdale International Airport.

ACCOMMODATIONS: 340 guest rooms and suites in Marina, Yacht Club and Country Club hotels, from 500 to 1,600 square feet.

DINING/ENTERTAINMENT: Thirteen restaurants and lounges including the Veranda, elegant dining overlooking promenade and pool gardens, dinner only; Monaco Dining Room, club-style menu featuring local seafood specialties; Ocean Club Grill; Sunset Cafe.

AMENITIES: 36 holes of golf; 24 tennis courts (18 lighted); three pro shops; full-service spa; marina; private beach club; limousine service; private helipad on property.

RATES: From $140 in low season to $275 in high season.

RESERVATIONS: Call (305) 937-0528.

Bonaventure Resort & Spa

QUESTION: WHAT DO AMERICAN Express, Chase Manhattan, Prudential Bache and IBM have in common? They've all sent their top executives and managers to the Bonaventure to have their batteries recharged and their engined re-tuned. This 500-room luxury resort not only caters to the everyday spa guest, but to the on-the-go "businessperson" as well.

Bonaventure also has much to offer the on-the-go golfer in the form of two 18-hole championship layouts: the Joe Lee-designed East Course (cited by *Golf* magazine as one of Florida's top 10), and the par-70 West Course.

East offers length (7,011 yards), a goodly number of water hazards (14 holes worth) and exceptionally fast-rolling greens. West, at only 6,200 yards, can be man-handled, er, person-handled with snappy iron play and a hot putter. (If you've got both of those working that day, even par is very, very possible.)

Dining at Bonaventure is an adventure in the waterfall-surrounded Renaissance Seafood Grill and casual in the Garden Restaurant, but don't overlook the Spa Dining Room, where the low-calorie, low-fat cuisine will surprise you with its flavor and presentation.

The Bonaventure regimen—including the services of the spa and the nutritious fare of the dining room—was once touted by spokesperson Linda Evans. Any *more* questions? ■

Bonaventure Resort & Spa
250 Racquet Club Road
Ft. Lauderdale, FL 33326

LOCATION: 20 minutes west of Ft. Lauderdale International Airport, 40 minutes from Miami.

ACCOMMODATIONS: 504 deluxe rooms and suites in nine four-story buildings, most with private terraces.

DINING/ENTERTAINMENT: Renaissance Seafood Grill, Continental and American specialties surrounded by waterfalls and a tropical garden; Garden Restaurant, breakfast, lunch and dinner in casual atmosphere; Spa Dining Room, flavorful, healthy cuisine.

AMENITIES: 36 holes of golf; 24-tennis-court racquet club with racquetball and squash; five swimming pools; Saddle Club equestrian center; skating and bowling nearby.

MEETING FACILITIES: 83,000-square-foot World Conference Center comprises three ballrooms, 10 meeting rooms, three board rooms and a 170-seat amphitheater.

RATES: Call for golf- and spa-package rates.

RESERVATIONS: Call (305) 389-3300.

Don Shula's Hotel & Golf Club

THE OAKLAND RAIDERS (WHO currently, and in all likelihood temporarily, reside in Los Angeles) are well recognized for their team motto, "Commitment to Excellence." But the phrase was actually coined in Miami in 1972 when the Don Shula-coached Dolphins went an astounding 17-0, winning the Super Bowl in both 1973 and '74.

I know that for sure. I was living in Miami at the time, and certain "acquaintances" of mine were involved in a gambling frenzy, betting on the Dolphins every week during "The Streak" (I believe they covered the spread 13 or 14 times). "Eddie," these acquaintances would implore every Saturday night, "put your money on the Dolphins this week. Shula's got this commitment to excellence and it's rubbed off on his players. They *can't* lose."

I, of course, thought that every week of the streak would be its last, and so every Saturday night I'd drop a little money on the Dolphins' opponents, figuring that sooner or later I'd be proved correct. Hmmm...

But that was then and this is now, 20 years later, and Shula has 300-plus NFL wins and has taken his teams to a record six Super Bowls, and it's a new me. And I say it's an almighty lock. Give the points and bet the mortgage. Attach Don Shula's name to any South Florida venture and it's going to work. Period. Especially when your starting out with a resort property which is already highly successful.

Shula knows football, and he knows how to travel (29 seasons in the league have taught him both). So it was a natural when he became an equity partner with The Graham Companies in the Miami Lakes Inn, Athletic Club and Golf Resort, lending his name and his expertise to the recently renovated and expanded 200-acre, 301-room property in Miami Lakes, just minutes from Miami International Airport.

This latest iteration of the resort, Don Shula's Hotel & Golf Club, offers dining in SHU'S All-Star Cafe, Florida's premier sports restaurant, and at Shula's Steak House, recently recognized by the Knife

& Fork Club as one of the 10 best in America. That is what's new.

What remains from the "olden" days is the 7,055-yard (6,500 yards from the regular tees), 18-hole golf course, opened in 1962 as the Miami Lakes Country Club. One-hundred-foot-tall trees block out the Florida sun and collect many an errant shot on this "mature" course, and water comes into play on eight of the holes, providing respite to the osprey, blue heron and wild parrots that abound on the property.

The signature hole is the 527-yard, par-5 ninth, a dogleg right with three tall trees guarding the bend in the fairway. Par is easily made if a well-struck tee shot is kept to the left. The inclination, however, is to cut off as much of the dogleg as possible, and it's a relatively safe assumption that these three trees have collected as many golf balls during the past 30 years as the range picker at your local club.

Other amenities at Shula's include a 2,080-yard, par-three executive course and a driving range/practice facility, both lighted until 10 p.m. for the late-arriving business traveler.

About the Steak House: You might think that a restaurant decorated with memorabilia celebrating the undefeated season would be, well, jock-like. Nothing could be further from the truth. White linen, fresh-cut flowers and the finest silver service give this room a club-like ambience that will surprise and delight you. And the cuisine scores big, from the 48-ounce porterhouse steak to the fresh local seafood (served in somewhat smaller portions, naturally) to the Maine lobster, you'll think you're dining in one of Miami's high-visibility, high-ticket eateries. (*Chez Shula's?*.... Nah.)

The resort also comprises a $7-million Athletic Club with nine lighted tennis courts, gymnasium, racquetball courts, whirlpools, aerobics and weight training, which is so state-of-the-art that the Dolphins conduct their off-season conditioning program there. (By the way, the Dolphins cheerleaders hone their considerable skills there, too.)

Shula calls the resort and the value to be found here the "Winning Edge." I'm not sure there's anyone out there qualified to dispute him. ■

DON SHULA'S HOTEL & GOLF CLUB — MIAMI LAKES, FLA.

LOCATION: 20 minutes northwest of Miami International Airport.

ACCOMMODATIONS: 201 guest rooms in the hotel; 100 guest rooms in the Golf Club overlooking the course.

DINING/ENTERTAINMENT: Shula's Steak House, award-winning steaks, seafood; SHU'S All-Star Cafe, informal, with big-screen sports TV; Center Court, lighter fare at the Athletic Club; The Bull Pen.

AMENITIES: 18 holes of golf; 18-hole lighted executive course; two swimming pools; fully equipped Athletic Club with weight training, aerobics; nine lighted tennis courts.

MEETING FACILITIES: Twenty-two rooms, 17,335 square feet accommodating 10-320.

RATES: Hotel and Golf Club rooms and suites from $89 to $199.

RESERVATIONS: Call (800) 24-SHULA.

Indian River Plantation

I KNOW THAT MANY GOLF "PURISTS" have a difficult time with courses that don't play 7,000 yards, don't have a slope rating of at least 145 and don't host a PGA, Senior PGA or LPGA Tour event. So those folks (you know who I'm talking to) probably won't appreciate the 4,042-yard, par-61 layout at Indian River Plantation Resort and Marina on Hutchinson Island in Stuart.

Although the two nines—River and Plantation—comprise 13 par-threes, four par-fours and a lone par-five, the course has enough water and sand to make it challenging for low handicappers as well as high. And considering that many of the resort guests are conference attendees, some of whom are playing for the first time, I appreciate the fact that I can get behind slower players and still make it around in under 3-1/2 hours.

But don't think you can blow into Indian River, card a 57 and get out of town. Scores in the low 60s are not uncommon, naturally, but with water in

play on 16 holes there will be enough lost balls to keep you from setting the course record.

The closing hole on the Plantation Course, at 495 yards, is in my opinion the most difficult, with water on the left of the tee and fairway bunkers strategically located on both sides of the landing area. The second shot must either carry more water fronting the green, or be laid up to the narrow right-hand forward corner of the fairway. The putting surface is well protected, and it's difficult to stop a 3- or 4-wood before it rolls into one of the surrounding sand bunkers. It's *so* reachable, though, that it's nearly impossible to resist the temptation. Go for it! There are at least four holes on this nine that force you to make birdie, so if you lose one to par on No. 9 you're probably still ahead of the game.

The resort's amenities are top notch, from its 13-court tennis complex to it's 77-slip marina on the Indian River, which offers a fuel dock, ship's store, washers and dryers, cable TV and telephone hook-ups. Available for private charter or regularly scheduled cruises is the *Island Princess*, an 84-foot, double-decker luxury river cruiser, which holds up to 150 passengers and plies the pristine waterways in the region.

While the hotel rooms are very comfortable, the one- and two-bedroom oceanfront suites with kitchens and private balconies are the preferred accommodations. The hotel rooms, however, have a delightful view of the marina, and the value these lodgings offer shouldn't be overlooked.

Scalawags is the most popular eatery at Indian River, but The Inlet, with seating for only 60, comes highly recommended. It is elegant and service oriented, and the Continental cuisine—which is its specialty—is well prepared and presented. The Porch offers casual indoor/outdoor dining overlooking the tennis complex, and The Emporium rounds out the facilities with its *very* casual atmosphere and all-day menu.

This a great little resort, top to bottom, and if you're golf *standards* won't allow you to play courses like those at Indian River, you need to rethink your position....immediately. ■

Indian River Plantation
555 N.E. Ocean Blvd., Hutchinson Island, Stuart, FL 34996

LOCATION: 45 minutes north of Palm Beach.

ACCOMMODATIONS: 200-room luxury hotel; 56 one- and two-bedroom oceanfront suites.

DINING/ENTERTAINMENT: Scalawags Restaurant, American and Continental cuisine overlooking marina; The Inlet, secluded, serving Continental cuisine for dinner only; The Porch, casual indoor/outdoor setting; The Emporium, breakfast and all-day menu; Scalawags Lounge; Gilbert's, lounge; 19th Hole.

AMENITIES: 18-hole (par-61) golf course with aqua driving range; 13 tennis courts (seven lighted); three swimming pools; outdoor spa; jogging; bicycling; private beach; deep-sea fishing; powerboat and jet ski rental; 84-foot, double-deck river cruiser; full-service marina (77 slips); kids programs.

MEETING FACILITIES: 15,000 square feet of divisible space including Plantation Ballroom, seating for 525 (400 banquet).

RATES: From $110 to $330.

RESERVATIONS: Call (800) 327-4960.

Longboat Key Club

ONE OF THE FIRST TOURISTS TO HIT the beach at Longboat Key was Hernando DeSoto, who arrived in 1539 and shortly thereafter made life so miserable for the residents they were forced to move inland. Obviously, not much has changed with tourism in the subsequent 450 years, but a great deal has changed at Longboat Key.

Longboat Key Club is a 1,000-acre resort, private club and residential community developed by Arvida Corp., the namesake of Arthur Vining Davis, founder of ALCOA. Davis purchased the property from the estate of John Ringling, who had before his death envisioned the area as the premier resort community on Florida's West Coast.

Today the Inn on the Beach at Longboat Key Club and its associated amenities are the fruition of the two men's dreams. The 221-room Inn is a perennial four-star/four-diamond award winner, and the resort's 18-hole golf course would make both Ringling and Davis proud.

Designed by Billy Mitchell and opened in 1960, the 6,890-yard, par-72 Islandside Golf Course borders the Gulf and plays around and through more than 5,000 palm trees and about as many water hazards. The fairways are lush, the greens well manicured and true. The course can play tough, so tourists with an attitude, like DeSoto, will enjoy the experience. ■

LONGBOAT KEY CLUB — LONGBOAT KEY, FLA.

LOCATION: 301 Gulf of Mexico Dr., Longboat Key, FL 34228; 10 min. from Sarasota.

ACCOMMODATIONS: 221 privately owned vacation suites overlooking the Gulf and the Islandside Golf Course.

DINING/ENTERTAINMENT: Island House, breakfast, lunch and dinner in an elegant tropical setting; The Grille Room, casual breakfast and lunch; Le Club, gourmet dining with music and dancing; Orchid Room.

AMENITIES: 18 holes of golf; 14 tennis courts (six lighted); swimming pools located throughout the property; Parcours track for jogging and exercise; 12 miles of Gulf beach; sailing; deep-sea fishing.

MEETING FACILITIES: Fully equipped conference rooms for groups of 15 to 200.

RATES: From $100 to $550.

RESERVATIONS: Call (813) 383-8821.

Palm-Aire Spa Resort

I REMEMBER THE DAY I CHECKED into Palm-Aire Spa Resort in Pompano Beach like it was yesterday. I walked in silence behind the bellman down the long hallway that led to my "wing." As he inserted the key into the door he turned slowly toward me and said in total solemnity, "Frank Sinatra stayed in this suite." That was it. That's all that was necessary. And by golly, any suite good enough for Frank Sinatra should certainly be good enough for me.

It was. Palm-Aire's accommodations are top-notch (Hey! George Steinbrenner and the Yankees stay here during spring training!) and its spa facilities are world-renowned. That's the part most people know about. What most of them don't know is that Palm-Aire has four excellent par-72 golf courses (two by George Fazio and one each from William Mitchell and Robert Von Hagge) and a par-60 executive course (also by Von Hagge) that are among the most highly regarded—by a knowledgable few—in South Florida .

A personal favorite is the Oaks Course, built by Fazio in 1971. Its tree-lined fairways require accuracy from the tee, but its large putting surfaces offer the opportunity to score well if your putter is working that day. On it I shot my best-ever Florida round: a 76 that needed only *23 putts* on the true-rolling greens. I don't know what Sinatra shot, but I know he didn't do it, er, my way.■

Palm-Aire Spa Resort
2501 Palm-Aire Drive North
Pompano Beach, FL 33069

LOCATION: 45 minutes north of Miami, 15 miles from Ft. Lauderdale International Airport.

ACCOMMODATIONS: 191 superior and deluxe one- and two-bedroom suites.

DINING/ENTERTAINMENT: Spa Dining Room, gourmet, calorie-controlled cuisine; Peninsula Dining Room, Continental fare; Palms Club House; Oaks Club House, casual atmosphere for lunch; Spa Lounge; Spa Pool Deck; Renaissance Pool and Garden.

AMENITIES: Five 18-hole golf courses (including one executive course); 37 tennis courts (six all-weather, lighted for night play); two swimming pools; 40,000-square-foot spa with world-class facilities and services; jogging track; squash; racquetball; private beach (five miles from property); two golf clubhouses; golf and tennis pro shops; boutiques for men and women.

RATES: 3 day/2 night packages available from approx. $280 per person; 8 day/7 night spa packages from approx. $2,000.

RESERVATIONS: Call (305) 972-3300.

Plantation Golf & Country Club

PRIMARILY A RESIDENTIAL COMMUNITY in south Sarasota County, the 1,300 Plantation Golf & Country Club encompasses nearly 900 condominiums, villas and single-family homes with an architectural theme reminiscent of Bermuda. The guest lodgings—200 of which are in the resort rental program—are interspersed throughout the two Ron Garl-designed golf courses, Bobcat and Panther.

Bobcat has been ranked among the top 50 courses in the state and features rolling hills, water in play on 16 holes (sound familiar?) and "blind" tee shots on 12 of them. Panther has two island greens and similar rolling terrain, but offers a number of elevated landing areas and tiered putting surfaces.

The centerpiece of the plantation is the luxurious clubhouse—which maintains the resort's Bermuda-style design theme—comprising a competition-size swimming pool, eight lighted Har-Tru tennis courts, golf and tennis pro shops, the Golf & Racquet Grill and The Manor restaurant, an elegant dining room serving Continental cuisine.

The residential side of the property features six different communities, ranging in price from approximately $100,000 to well over $300,000 on lakeview and golf-view half-acre lots.

If you're planning a trip to the Plantation you'd better pack an extra suitcase. Some visitors have vacationed here and never were heard from again. ■

Plantation Golf & Country Club
500 Rockley Boulevard
Venice, FL 34293

LOCATION: 45 minutes from Sarasota/Bradenton Airport via Interstate 75.

ACCOMMODATIONS: 200 luxury condominiums and villas in resort rental program.

DINING/ENTERTAINMENT: The Manor Restaurant, Continental cuisine in elegant clubhouse setting, Tuesday through Saturday; Golf & Racquet Grill; Manor Lounge, open Monday through Saturday, featuring live entertainment Thursday, Friday and Saturday.

AMENITIES: Two 18-hole golf courses (Ron Garl); eight-court tennis complex (lighted) including 1,300-seat stadium court, pro shop and locker rooms; competition-size swimming pool; 45 acres of lakes for freshwater fishing, Gulf fishing minutes away; fitness trail; biking.

RATES: Call for seasonal rates and available packages.

RESERVATIONS: Call (813) 493-2500.

Places To Play

Southern Florida

Avon Park

Pinecrest On Lotela
2250 S. Little Lake Bonnet Rd.
Avon Park, FL 33825
(813) 453-7555
TYPE OF FACILITY: Public
NO. OF HOLES: 18
DESIGN: Traditional
YARDAGE: 5,350-6,449
PAR: 72
PEAK RATES: $16 for 18 holes. Cart included.

Boca Raton

Boca Raton Municipal G.C.
8111 Golf Course Road
Boca Raton, FL 33434
(407) 483-6278
TYPE OF FACILITY: Public
NO. OF HOLES: 18 + 9 executive
DESIGN: Traditional
YARDAGE: 5,306-6,593
PAR: 72
PEAK RATES: $17 for 18 holes. Cart included.

Boca Raton (cont.)

Sandlefoot Country Club
1400 Country Club Dr.
Boca Raton, FL 33428
(305) 426-0880
TYPE OF FACILITY: Semi-private
NO. OF HOLES: 18
DESIGN: Traditional
YARDAGE: 5,325-6,625
PAR: 72
PEAK RATES: $44 for 18 holes. Cart included.

Southwind Golf Club
19557 Lyons Road
Boca Raton, FL 33434
(407) 483-1305
TYPE OF FACILITY: Public
NO. OF HOLES: 18
DESIGN: Links
YARDAGE: 4,407-5,643
PAR: 71
PEAK RATES: $26 for 18 holes. Cart included.

Boynton Beach

Cypress Creek Country Club
9400 N. Military Trail
Boynton Beach, FL 33436
(407) 732-4202
Type of Facility: Semi-private
No. of Holes: 18
Design: Traditional
Yardage: 5,500-6,800
Par: 72
Peak Rates: $40. Cart included.

Boynton Beach Municipal G.C.
8020 Jog Rd.
Boynton Beach, FL 33437
(407) 969-2200
Type of Facility: Public
No. of Holes: 18 + 9 executive
Design: Traditional
Yardage: 5,089-6,331
Par: 71
Peak Rates: $30. Cart included.

Cape Coral

Coral Oaks Golf Club
1800 N.W. 28th Avenue
Cape Coral, FL 33909
Type of Facility: Public
No. of Holes: 18
Design: Links
Yardage: 4,803-6,623
Par: 72
Peak Rates: $45 for 18 holes. Cart included.

Cape Coral Golf & Tennis Resort
4003 Palm Tree Blvd.
Cape Coral, FL 33904
(813) 542-3191
Type of Facility: Resort
No. of Holes: 18
Design: Traditional
Yardage: 5,488-6,649
Par: 72
Peak Rates: $49.50. Cart included.

Coral Gables

The Biltmore Golf Club
1210 Anastasia Ave.
Coral Gables, FL 33134
(305) 460-5366
Type of Facility: Public
No. of Holes: 18
Design: Traditional
Yardage: 6,652
Par: 71
Peak Rates: $51 including cart.

Deerfield Beach

Deer Creek Golf Club
2801 Country Club Blvd.
Deerfield Beach, FL 33442
(305) 421-5550
Type of Facility: Semi-private
No. of Holes: 18
Design: Traditional
Yardage: 5,300-6,700
Par: 72
Peak Rates: $65. Cart included.

Del Ray Beach

Villa Del Ray Golf Club
6200 Villa Del Ray
Del Ray Beach, FL 33484
(407) 498-1444
Type of Facility: Semi-private
No. of Holes: 18
Design: Traditional
Yardage: 5,442-6,151
Par: 71
Peak Rates: $38. Cart included.

Englewood

Lemon Bay Golf Club
5800 Placida Rd.
Englewood, FL 34224
(813) 697-4190
Type of Facility: Semi-private
No. of Holes: 18
Design: Marshland
Yardage: 4,955-6,170
Par: 71
Peak Rates: $35. Cart included.

Ft. Lauderdale

Arrowhead Country Club
8201 S.W. 24th Street
Ft. Lauderdale, FL 33324
(305) 475-8200
Type of Facility: Semi-private
No. of Holes: 18
Design: Traditional
Yardage: 4,988-6,506
Par: 71
Peak Rates: $38. Cart included.

Rolling Hills Hotel & Conf. Center
3501 West Rolling Hills Circle
Ft. Lauderdale, FL 33328
(305) 475-0400
Type of Facility: Resort
No. of Holes: 27
Design: Traditional
Yardage: 5,582-6,905
Par: 72
Peak Rates: $45. Cart included.

Ft. Myers

Eastwood Golf Course
4600 Bruce Head Lane
Ft. Myers, FL 33905
(813) 275-4848
Type of Facility: Public
No. of Holes: 18
Design: Traditional
Yardage: 5,116-6,772
Par: 72
Peak Rates: $25. $37.50 with cart.

Ft. Myers Country Club
1445 Hill Avenue
Ft. Myers, FL 33901
(813) 936-2457
Type of Facility: Public
No. of Holes: 18
Design: Traditional
Yardage: 5,396-6,414
Par: 71
Peak Rates: $25. $37.50 with cart.

Ft. Myers (cont.)

Gateway Golf Club
11360 Championship Drive
Ft. Myers, FL 33913
(813) 561-1010
TYPE OF FACILITY: Semi-private
NO. OF HOLES: 18
DESIGN: Links
YARDAGE: 5,323-6,974
PAR: 72
PEAK RATES: $75 including cart.

Port La Belle Inn & C.C.
1 Oxbox Drive
Port La Belle, FL 33935
TYPE OF FACILITY: Resort
NO. OF HOLES: 18
DESIGN: Traditional
YARDAGE: 5,005-6,900
PAR: 72
PEAK RATES: $45 for 18 holes. Cart included.

Ft. Pierce

Gator Trace Country Club
4302 Gator Trace Dr.
Ft. Pierce, FL 34982
(407) 464-0407
TYPE OF FACILITY: Semi-private
NO. OF HOLES: 18
DESIGN: Links
YARDAGE: 4,573-6,013
PAR: 70
PEAK RATES: $20. Cart included.

Indian Hills Golf & C.C.
1600 S. 3rd Street
Ft. Pierce, FL 34950
(407) 461-9620
TYPE OF FACILITY: Semi-private resort
NO. OF HOLES: 18
DESIGN: Traditional
YARDAGE: 5,232-6,300
PAR: 72
PEAK RATES: $27. Cart included.

Hollywood

Hollywood Golf & C.C.
1650 Johnson Street
Hollywood, FL 33020
(305) 927-1751
TYPE OF FACILITY: Semi-private
NO. OF HOLES: 18
DESIGN: Traditional
YARDAGE: 6,200-6,550
PAR: 70
PEAK RATES: $33. Cart included.

Homestead

Redlands Golf & Country Club
24451 S.W. 177th Ave.
Homestead, FL 33090
TYPE OF FACILITY: Semi-private
NO. OF HOLES: 18
DESIGN: Traditional
YARDAGE: 5,800-6,600
PAR: 72
PEAK RATES: $42 for 18 holes. Cart included.

Jupiter

Indian Creek Golf Club
1800 Central Blvd.
Jupiter, FL 33458
(407) 747-6262
TYPE OF FACILITY: Public
NO. OF HOLES: 18
DESIGN: Traditional
YARDAGE: 5,150-6,155
PAR: Men: 70. Ladies: 71.
PEAK RATES: $40 for 18 holes. Cart included.

Key Biscayne

The Links at Key Biscayne
6700 Crandon Blvd.
Key Biscayne, FL 33149
(305) 361-9129
TYPE OF FACILITY: Semi-private
NO. OF HOLES: 18
DESIGN: Desert
YARDAGE: 3,393-4,131
PAR: 65
PEAK RATES: $23 for 18 holes. Cart optional.

Key Largo

Ocean Reef Club
31 Ocean Reef Drive
Key Largo, FL 33037
(305) 367-2611
TYPE OF FACILITY: Resort
NO. OF HOLES: 36
DESIGN: Marshland
YARDAGE: 5,400-6,400
PAR: 71
PEAK RATES: $60. $79 with cart.

Lehigh

Lehigh Resort
225 East Joel Blvd.
Lehigh, FL 33936
(813) 369-2121
TYPE OF FACILITY: Resort
NO. OF HOLES: 36
DESIGN: Traditional
YARDAGE: 5,316-6,949
PAR: 72 (South course). 71 (North)
PEAK RATES: $27. $52 with cart.

Naples

Marco Shores Country Club
1450 Mainsail Drive
Naples, FL 33961
(813) 394-2581
TYPE OF FACILITY: Public
NO. OF HOLES: 18
DESIGN: Traditional
YARDAGE: 5,634-6,879
PAR: 72
PEAK RATES: $45. Cart included.

Naples Beach Hotel & Golf Club
851 Gulf Shore Blvd. N.
Naples, FL 33940
(813) 261-2222
TYPE OF FACILITY: Public
NO. OF HOLES: 18
DESIGN: Traditional
YARDAGE: 5,315-6,462
PAR: 72
PEAK RATES: $75. Cart included.

North Ft. Myers

Lochmoor Country Club
3911 Orange Grove
North Ft. Myers, FL 33903
(813) 995-0501
TYPE OF FACILITY: Semi-private
NO. OF HOLES: 18
DESIGN: Traditional
YARDAGE: 5,765-6,940
PAR: 72
PEAK RATES: $44. Cart included.

North Miami Beach

Presidential Country Club
19650 N.E. 18th Ave.
North Miami Beach, FL 33179
(305) 933-5266
TYPE OF FACILITY: Public
NO. OF HOLES: 18
DESIGN: Traditional
YARDAGE: 5,794-6,964
PAR: 72
PEAK RATES: $32. Cart included.

Pembroke Pines

Grand Palms Golf & C.C.
110 Grand Palms Drive
Pembroke Pines, FL 33027
(800) 327-9246
TYPE OF FACILITY: Semi-private
NO. OF HOLES: 18
DESIGN: Marshland
YARDAGE: 5,245-6,757
PAR: 72
PEAK RATES: $40. Cart included.

Pembroke Lakes G. & Racq. Club
10500 Taft Street
Pembroke Pines, FL 33026
(305) 431-4144
TYPE OF FACILITY: Semi-private
NO. OF HOLES: 18
DESIGN: Traditional
YARDAGE: 5,811-6,646
PAR: 72
PEAK RATES: $34. Cart included.

Plantation

Jacaranda Golf Club
9200 W. Broward
Plantation, FL 33324
TYPE OF FACILITY: Semi-private
NO. OF HOLES: 36
DESIGN: Traditional
YARDAGE: 5,274-6,668 (East) 5,658-7,170 (West)
PAR: 72
PEAK RATES: $65. Cart included.

Ponte Gorda

Burnt Store Marina Resort
3150 Matecombe Key Road
Ponte Gorda, FL 33955
(800) 237-4255
TYPE OF FACILITY: Resort
NO. OF HOLES: 27
DESIGN: Traditional
YARDAGE: 3,069-4,000
PAR: 60
PEAK RATES: $24. Cart included.

Royal Palm Beach

Royal Palm Beach C.C.
900 Royal Palm Beach Blvd.
Royal Palm Beach, FL 33411
(407) 798-6430
Type of Facility: Public
No. of Holes: 18
Design: Traditional
Yardage: 4,724-7,067
Par: 72
Peak Rates: $16 for 18 holes. Cart optional.

Sanibel Island

Sundial Beach & Tennis Resort
949 Sandcastle Road
Sanibel Island, FL 33957
(813) 472-2535
Type of Facility: Semi-private resort
No. of Holes: 18
Design: Traditional
Yardage: 5,093-5,715
Par: 70
Peak Rates: $70 for 18 holes. Cart included.

Sunrise

Sunrise Country Club
7400 N.W. 24th Place
Sunrise, FL 33313
(305) 742-4333
Type of Facility: Semi-private
No. of Holes: 18
Design: Traditional
Yardage: 5,311-6,668
Par: 72
Peak Rates: $20. Cart included.

Vero Beach

Vista Royal Golf & C.C.
100 Woodland Drive
Vero Beach, FL 32962
(407) 562-8110
Type of Facility: Semi-private
No. of Holes: 27
Design: Marshland
Yardage: 4,668-5,758
Par: 70
Peak Rates: $35. Cart included.

West Palm Beach

Emerald Dunes Golf Course
2100 Emerald Dunes Dr.
West Palm Beach, FL 33411
Type of Facility: Semi-private
No. of Holes: 18
Design: Traditional
Yardage: 4,676-7,006
Par: 72
Peak Rates: $115 for 18 holes. Cart included.

West Palm Beach Country Club
7001 Parker Ave.
West Palm Beach, FL 33405
(407) 582-2019
Type of Facility: Public
No. of Holes: 18
Design: Traditional
Yardage: 6,523
Par: 72
Peak Rates: $40. Cart included.

The Bahamas

I'M NOT SURE WHY THE BAHAMAS ARE SO OFTEN OVERLOOKED as a golf destination by the traveling American golfer. I can't tell you how many times I've struck up a conversation on an airplane to the islands and had the fellow next to me say, "Gee. Do they have golf there?" Hey, buddy! Wake up and smell the capucino. It's the '90s—they have golf *everywhere*. Thankfully, since the Bahamas were named an official destination of the PGA Tour in the late 1980s, savvy golfers have begun loading up their clubs when they make the 30- to 60-minute flight from practically any East Coast hub to any of the islands in the chain. You can bet it won't be very long before everyone else catches on.

If you were to visit a different Bahamian island every day you wouldn't return to your point of origin for almost two years. That's a lot of territory to cover, and I assume most of us are in the same boat and really can't give up the two years just now. That's why it's best to shop for the *type* of resort you'd like to visit. And I mean only for *this* particular trip. You may be looking for a private little slice of paradise where you can tee it up in the morning, play a few sets of tennis in the afternoon, have a cocktail on the patio and an early dinner and be in bed by 9. That sounds a lot like Cotton Bay Club on Eleuthera, where you can do all of these things in the relative seclusion that comes from *all* the guests having the same interests. (In other words, I wouldn't bring my teenagers with me if they can't exist without a boom box and MTV for a couple of days.)

But although that may be exactly what you're looking for this time, it doesn't necessarily mean that you're interested in making "seclusion" a steady diet. Nightlife in the Bahamas is about as exciting as there is, from the venerable casino at the Bahamas Princess (left) to the casino and entertainment complex at Paradise Island Resort. Or you can find a mix—the best of both worlds—at resorts like Atlantik Beach (above) where many of the activities (day and night) are located nearby rather than immediately outside your hotel room. Whatever you're looking for, whenever you're looking for it—that's what a vacation in the Bahamas is all about.

Transportation options are as diverse as the resorts you'll be visiting. Your travel agent may book a reservation for you with a major carrier, or perhaps arrange to have you placed on the manifest of the charter planes that the casinos sponsor for their high-rollers. You can travel on a cruise ship, charter yacht, bare-boat yacht or seaplane. The alternatives are limited only by your imagination.

One final word, regarding the weather: Perfect.

See you there.

Cotton Bay Club

"Where who's-who goes barefoot in the Bahamas"

I'M SURE YOU'VE DONE THIS SAME thing countless times: invite a couple of your closest friends for a few days at your place to play golf, wine and dine at your favorite restaurant and spend time relaxing on the beach or hanging a line over the side of your boat. When it's over you ship your guests home refreshed and ready to face the rigors of the business world in which they operate. That is precisely what Juan Tripp had in mind when he founded the Cotton Bay Club on the island of Eleuthera in the Bahamas....in a manner of speaking.

The only difference between you and the late Mr. Tripp is that he would fly his friends to his 450-acre, ocean-front Bahamian resort on a Pan Am Yankee Clipper, the *Cotton Bay Special*, where his guests would stay in one of 77 club rooms and individual cottages, play the only Robert Trent Jones-designed golf course in the Bahamas, luxuriate on the crescent-shaped, white-sand beach (one of the most scenic and undisturbed in the entire island chain) and dine outdoors on island specialties and the finest Continental cuisine money could buy.

Indeed, money was of little consequence to Tripp, the founder of Pan Am, who spent a good deal of his time seeking out the "nooks and crannies" of the world as vacation grounds for his exceptionally wealthy acquaintances. Tripp had the resort built in 1957 on land originally owned by ALCOA magnate Arthur Vining Davis, who in turn sold it to Tripp, who in turn asked his friend Trent Jones to design the course. What a country!

Fortunately this fine resort is no longer private, and guests from around the world have for the past 30 years enjoyed the telephoneless, televisionless, trafficless serenity available at this island hideaway just an hour's flight from Miami and 30 minutes from Nassau. And with the club-operated Davis Harbour Marina only 4.5 miles from the resort, *yachtspersons* find it an attractive stopover during their annual Bahamian island cruise.

Cotton Bay has been a landmark on the Caribbean golfing map since the completion of the facility, but focus has been more acute since the Bahamas was named an official destination of the PGA Tour in 1989. Adding to the resort's overall visibility has been the often-photographed 546-yard, par-5 sixth, one of the select holes in all of golf that is as beautiful from green to tee as it is vice-versa.

This dogleg-right plays outward from the main hotel building and wraps around the most scenic stretch of the incredibly scenic bay. On most days a long, fading tee shot will give you the impression that the green is reachable in two. It's not. The coastal breezes swirl incessantly behind the putting surface, and the same wind that helped bend your drive around the corner will now knock down your second shot long before you expect. A 1-iron struck perfectly, I thought, dropped harmlessly about 50 yards short. My playing partner, a complete stranger, laughed heartily up until the moment he launched a 3-wood that came to rest about three feet in front of my ball. So much for club selection, and so much for traditional golf etiquette.

The second most beautiful hole on this course follows immediately thereafter: the 163-yard, par-3 seventh, a Pebble Beach-like hole that—much like the famous No. 7 on the Monterey peninsula—plays anywhere from a 9-iron to a 2-iron, depending on the wind. Oddly (since the holes play in opposite directions), a following wind on No. 6 does not necessarily mean a hindering wind on No. 7. In fact, since the holes are on different sides of the tiny peninsula, and at markedly different elevations for so short a distance, you can be wind-assisted on both. But don't get too excited. At over 7,000 yards, with a

Below: The villas at Cotton Bay Club are comfortably elegant, with interior design as colorful as the gardens that surround them. Above right: On course for the seaside sixth and seventh holes.

mind-boggling 129 bunkers and 13 water hazards (in addition to the Caribbean Sea, that is) and the aforementioned wind, getting past six and seven with pars is only the beginning.

This course will test your skill and your patience from start to finish, although if you're striking the ball well that day you can pretty much put it on cruise control between holes 10 and 14. The par-three 15th, at 201-yards, is a nail-biter, but still only a subtle prelude to the relatively short but overtly deadly 508-yard, par-five 16th. With water in front of the tee and running the length of the hole on the left side, your initial thought is grab your driver and rip it down the right. Wrong! Eight of the 129 bunkers line the starboard side of No. 16, and my sole birdie in four attempts came with this club selection: 5-iron, 4-iron, pitching wedge. This may raise a few eyebrows on the tee, but we all know we shouldn't let our ego get in the way of our score, don't we?

After golf, kicking back on the beach is the favored preoccupation at Cotton Bay, then it's on to a few cocktails in the lounge or poolside and dinner outdoors in a candle-lit setting with exquisite cuisine and service to match.

A moonlight stroll on the beach alongside the crashing, phosphorescent surf rounds out the day perfectly. This obviously is what Juan Tripp had in mind when he first envisioned Cotton Bay.

So instead of inviting your friends to your place next time, why not take them to Cotton Bay? You may not be able to fly them there on your private jet, as did Mr. Tripp, but then again, when they finally leave you won't get stuck changing the sheets. ■

COTTON BAY CLUB — ELEUTHERA, BAHAMAS

LOCATION: Twelve miles south of Rock Sound International Airport.

ACCOMMODATIONS: 77 guest rooms and cottages, all with private patios.

DINING/ENTERTAINMENT: Indoor/outdoor terrace dining overlooking the pool and ocean, serving island specialties and Continental cuisine, extensive wine list; music and dancing Wednesdays and Saturdays; guitar music with dinner seven nights; lounge and poolside cocktail service.

AMENITIES: 18 holes of golf; four all-weather tennis courts; fresh-water swimming pool; snorkeling, Sunfish sailing; winsurfing; bicycling. Arrangements may be made for scuba diving, deep-sea fishing and car rentals.

MEETING FACILITIES: 2,105 square feet of space accommodating groups from six to 80.

RATES: Vary by season; from $135 to $350.

RESERVATIONS: Call (800) 334-3523.

Paradise Island Resort & Casino

Home is where the heat, er, the heart is

FULLY HALF OF THE TRAVEL ARTICLES you'll read this year will extol the virtues of vacationing in a resort "that reminds you so much of home." That's fine. I like where I live, too, and there certainly is a place in my heart—and my schedule—for vacationing somewhere very much like it.

Paradise Island Resort & Casino is just such a place, where the peace and serenity of the surroundings make you feel as if you've never left your own neighborhood . . . Not!

Paradise Island is nothing like home, unless you live a lot harder and a lot faster than most. From the moment you cross the Gulf Stream and enter the turquoise-blue Bahamian waters, step into the bustling lobby of the resort, walk onto the wide, white-sand beach, or set foot in the 30,000-square-foot casino, you are well aware that home was never, ever like this. Which is one reason the Bahamas hosts nearly 3.5-million visitors a year.

Of course, you could visit a different Bahamian island every day for about two years and never set foot in the same place twice, and that is an admirable quest. But Paradise Island, just across the bridge from Nassau on New Providence Island is, especially for golfers, the perfect place to begin. The Bahamas have been named an official destination of the PGA Tour (we're not quite sure exactly what that means), and the Paradise Island Golf Club is, I believe, among the top ten courses in the Caribbean (although at only 50 miles off the Florida coast, the Bahamas are really in the Atlantic).

This Dick Wilson-designed seaside gem plays nearly 6,800 yards from the championship tees to a par of 72—from the regular tees just over 6,400 yards. What it lacks in length is made up for in bunkering (a minimum of five per hole), and water, which comes into play on no fewer than 13 holes. The holes are named for tropical trees like Sapodilla, Ju Ju, Guava and Gooseberry. To be honest, I wouldn't recognize a Tamarind tree if I walked into one, but the hole that bears its name, the 154-yard, par-3 sixth, is one of my personal favorites in the islands.

Tamarind should be a well-struck 5-iron on a normal day under normal circumstances, but in the Bahamas there is little that is "normal," and with the hole

practically surrounded by the crashing surf, a prevailing wind of 25 to 30 m.p.h., party boats with live goombay music, sailboats, waterskiers and parasailers circling offshore, and the distraction of the course's natural beauty, club selection becomes almost whimsical. No. 6 Tamarind and No. 7 Chickcharnee (a 413-yard, slightly uphill dogleg left, hard against the runway of Paradise Island Airport) have been nicknamed "The Devil's Half Acre," and as you walk to the tee of No. 8 you'll most likely be considering an afternoon of shuffleboard and rum punches.

Two more thoroughly enjoyable and exceptionally memorable holes are the 467-yard, par-five 13th (Hog Plum), and the 157-yard, par-three 14th (Coca Plum). Thirteen, "The Hog," as it came to be affectionately known in our group, has water left and right and bunkering in the landing area and around the green. This hole usually plays into the teeth of the wind, although the breeze swirls, most often after the ball already has been launched.

Coca Plum's championship tee box was under repair on the day we played, and at a paltry 120 yards from the forward tees it looked to be a pushover. Again, the prevailing winds wreak havoc with club selection, and five strokes later, with putter back in bag and ball coming to rest in the Atlantic as far as it could be thrown, we were already looking for-

In addition to the Resort & Casino, the property comprises the Paradise Paradise resort, below, and the Ocean Club Golf & Tennis Resort, above right.

ward to the evening's entertainment.

Fortunately, this is the *home* of entertainment, beginning with dinner in one of the 12 gourmet restaurants on the property. One of our favorites was Cafe Martinique, "Paris in Paradise" with wall-to-wall etched glass windows and candlelit terraces, serving a full French menu and boasting a wine list of considerable dimension. Another was Villa D'Este, with the best fettucine this side of the Italian lake resort for which is is named.

One other, Coyaba, deserves special mention. The atmosphere here is tropical, with a torchlight chandelier and wingback rattan chairs and little umbrellas in the drinks (You don't get that at home, do you?). The cuisine in Coyaba is a blend of Chinese, Polynesian and Szechuan, and I distinctly remember beads of sweat forming on my brow from the sweet and sour sauce and hot mustard.

Also at the resort you'll find no fewer than 12 nightclubs, bars and lounges offering music for every taste, from island music in the casino bar to the 116-speaker disco sound in Club Pastiche to the gaudy, glitzy show tunes in Le

Cabaret Theatre, which has an adults-only Las Vegas-style revue. There's also the Jokers Wild Comedy Club, featuring well-known comedians from the U.S. Then it's on to the casino, with its slot machines, blackjack, roulette, baccarat and "Salon Prive," the private room for high-rollers.

The following day it's back to the beach, the tennis courts, the golf course, to begin anew. Indeed, be it ever so humble, this is no place like home. ■

PARADISE ISLAND RESORT & CASINO — PARADISE ISLAND, BAHAMAS

LOCATION: 20 minutes from Nassau Airport; two minutes from Paradise Island Airport.

ACCOMMODATIONS: 1,200 guest rooms and suites at the Resort & Casino; 100 rooms at Paradise Paradise resort; 71 rooms and suites at the Ocean Club Golf & Tennis Resort.

DINING/ENTERTAINMENT: More than 35 facilities; 12 gourmet and specialty restaurants including Cafe Martinique, The Bahamian Club, Coyaba and Villa D'Este; Le Cabaret Theatre.

AMENITIES: Eighteen holes of golf; water-sports center including windsurfing, snorkeling, sailing; 21 tennis courts; fitness center; children's camp; duty-free shopping; casino.

MEETING FACILITIES: 50,000 square feet; two ballrooms accommodating 50 to 2,600.

RATES: From $130 to $875 at all three resorts.

RESERVATIONS: Call (800) 321-3000 or call the resort directly at (809) 363-3000.

Atlantik Beach Resort

THE ATLANTIK BEACH RESORT ON Grand Bahama Island is a perfect example of the "all, or nothing at all" approach visitors may take in the Bahamas. Situated on the world-famous Lucaya Beach—a short but costly taxi ride from the airport—fronting the emerald-green waters of the island chain, Atlantik Beach offers plenty of things to do (if you're so inclined), from snorkeling and scuba to sailing, windsurfing, parasailing, swimming and practically anything and everything else aquatic. Nearby there's tennis, bicycle and motor scooter rentals—please, take the bike and keep it on the path—a casino, a yacht harbor, deep-sea and coastal fishing and the Bahamian national pastime: shopping.

But because so many of these activities are "off-campus," the resort is a perfect getaway for those who really want to relax. The beach is peaceful (and beautiful), the accommodations are, if not luxurious, tastefully comfortable (the additional amenities of the deluxe room cost no more than many other resorts' standard features), and the dining is private and tasty in Alfredo's, an Italian specialty restaurant with seating for only 50.

But whether you dine there or in the highly recommended Arawak Dining Room on the golf course really doesn't matter. At Atlantik Beach Resort you can do whatever you feel like whenever you feel like it. Once you get here the meter stops running. ■

Atlantik Beach Resort
P.O. Box F-531
Grand Bahama Island

LOCATION: 35 minutes by air from Miami, 60 minutes by air from Orlando.

ACCOMMODATIONS: 120 standard, superior and deluxe rooms; 52 one- to three-bedroom apartments with kitchen or kitchenette.

DINING/ENTERTAINMENT: Arawak Dining Room, French gourmet cuisine situated on the golf course for lunch and dinner; Alfredo's, Italian specialties for dinner only; Butterfly, indoor/outdoor for breakfast, lunch and dinner; Yellow Elder Bar, live entertainment nightly; Obediah's Pool Bar, island drink specialties and snacks on the beach; Hall of Mirrors, banquets.

AMENITIES: 18-hole golf course (Lucaya Golf & Country Club); swimming pool; water sports including sailing, windsurfing, snorkeling, parasailing, beach parties; table tennis. Close by: six tennis courts; bicycle rental; deep-sea fishing; shopping center; casino.

RATES: From $90 to $300 per night.

RESERVATIONS: Call (809) 373-1444.

Divi Bahamas Beach Resort

MENTION NEW PROVIDENCE ISLAND and many people think of Nassau and nearby Paradise Island, as well they should. That's where the "name" resorts are located, and that's where the cruise ships make port daily. But tucked away on the island's southwestern shore is Divi Bahamas Beach Resort & Country Club, offering a Joe Lee-designed golf course and seclusion that borders on hermitage.

Divi Bahamas comprises nearly 200 acres of tropical luxury, including its own half-mile stretch of private beach and another five miles worth immediately adjacent, oceanfront accommodations with private terrace or balcony, and all the amenities and activities you would expect from a Divi Resort.

The golf course has been a Bahamian favorite for years, and at 6,800 yards—and usually playing directly into the prevailing winds—the layout demands hefty tee shots, carefully crafted approaches and a putter with legs—getting it down can be difficult, especially in late afternoon when the greens are dry and rolling at the same speed as linoleum.

There is also a small yet comprehensive tennis center, perhaps the best scuba and snorkeling within 100 miles, and an air of intimacy that necessitates traveling with your significant other. It's so (dare I say it) *romantic* here, I get warm and fuzzy just writing about it. The next time someone mentions New Providence Island, guess what I'll be thinking... ■

Divi Bahamas Beach Resort
P.O. Box N-8191 Nassau
New Providence, Bahamas

LOCATION: Southwest shore of New Providence Island, 10 minutes from Nassau Airport.

ACCOMMODATIONS: 250 superior and oceanfront luxury guest rooms.

DINING/ENTERTAINMENT: Papagayo, seasonal restaurant offering Bahamian and Continental cuisine in a tropical, elegant atmosphere; Casuarina, breakfast, lunch and dinner in a casual setting featuring island and American specialties. Pavilion bar, all-day refreshments; Pool Bar; Duffer's Bar, open until 1 a.m.

AMENITIES: 18-hole golf course (Joe Lee); four all-weather tennis courts (lighted); two swimming pools; all water sports including snorkeling, scuba, windsurfing, waterskiing and sunfish sailing; half-mile private beach; golf and tennis pro shops; Vita course.

MEETING FACILITIES: Accommodates 100 theater style.

RATES: Call for rates and packages.

RESERVATIONS: Call (809) 362-4391.

Bahamas Princess Resort & Casino

THE DISTINCTIVE MOORISH DESIGN of the casino at the Bahamas Princess Resort & Casino makes it probably the most recognizable of any in the world. But the 20,000-square-foot gaming area pales in comparison to the acreage of great golf at the resort, two 18-hole courses from the by now familiar tandem of Dick Wilson and Joe Lee. It's apparent these two had the Bahamian/Caribbean golf concession in the late 1950s and '60s, and no wonder—their designs are a fair test for every level of player (prerequisite for a resort), and they always seemed to take exceptional advantage of the terrain they had to work with, no matter how little or how much design flexibility it offered.

Wilson's Emerald Golf Course was opened in 1964, and to this day is considered by many (and rightfully so) to be the toughest test on Grand Bahama. Water is often and meaningfully in play, and the greens have enough slope in them to make even a two-footer *not* a sure thing. Lee's Ruby course isn't as long as the 7,000-yard Emerald, but it too has water on all fronts and more bunkers (in direct play, anyway) than many other resort designs.

The Princess features the largest freshwater pool on the island, and other amenities include tennis, all water sports and the venerable Princess Casino, the one thing in the Bahamas, apparently, that's not a Wilson/Lee design. ■

Bahamas Princess Resort & Casino
P.O. Box F-2623
Freeport, Grand Bahama Island

LOCATION: 35 minutes by air from Miami, 60 minutes by air from Orlando.

ACCOMMODATIONS: Princess Tower, 400 rooms including 19 suites; Princess Country Club, 565 rooms including 15 suites.

DINING/ENTERTAINMENT: Guanahani's, Bahamian and international specialties; Rib Room, gourmet steak house; Morgan's Bluff, Bahamian seafood specialties; La Trattoria, casual Italian fare; Crown Room, Continental gourmet cuisine; Patio; John B; Lemon Peel; Garden Cafe; 10 lounges with a variety of specialties and entertainment.

AMENITIES: 36 holes of golf; 12 tennis courts (lighted); two swimming pools, nearby beach club; all water sports; fitness center; car rental; casino.

MEETING FACILITIES: More than 42,000 square feet of flexible function space.

RATES: From $150 to $350 per night.

RESERVATIONS: Call (809) 352-9661.

Places To Play

The Bahamas

Abaco

Treasure Cay Golf & Country Club
Treasure Cay
Abaco, Bahamas
(809) 367-2570
TYPE OF FACILITY: Public
NO. OF HOLES: 18
DESIGN: Traditional
YARDAGE: 5,690-6,965
PAR: 72
PEAK RATES: $40 for 18. Cart $25. Club rental $12 for 18 or $7.50 for nine. Walking encouraged.
ARCHITECT: Dick Wilson
COMMENTS: Narrow fairways.

Grand Bahama

Fortune Hill Golf & Country Club
Freeport, Grand Bahama
(809) 373-4500
TYPE OF FACILITY: Semi-private
NO. OF HOLES: Nine
DESIGN: Traditional
YARDAGE: 3,102-3,458
PAR: 36
PEAK RATES: $20 for 18. $12 for nine. Cart for 1 or 2 persons $26 for 18 and $18 for nine. Club rental $13 for 18 and $8 for nine. Walking allowed.
ARCHITECT: Joe Lee

Nassau/New Providence

Crystal Palace Hotel & Golf Club
Cable Beach
Nassau, Bahamas
TYPE OF FACILITY: Resort
NO. OF HOLES: 18
DESIGN: Traditional
YARDAGE: 7,040
PAR: 72
PEAK RATES: $20 for 18 (guest). $28 for 18 (non-guest). $12 for nine (guest). $16 for nine (non-guest). Cart $30 for 18 and $16 for nine.
COMMENTS: The $130-million, 900,000-square-foot Crystal Palace offers 1,559 guest rooms.

The Caribbean

I THINK IT RATHER REMARKABLE THAT SO MANY KNOWLEDGABLE golfers, even those that travel far and frequently to play the game, still think of Caribbean golf as something to be tolerated when there's nothing else to do; to be played on courses that have oiled-sand putting surfaces and no recognizable fairways.

Quite the opposite is true. European vacationers have for years enjoyed first-class golf facilities in the islands, relatively unencumbered by the weight of the American golfing public.

Lately, however, the islands have become popular destinations for American travelers as well. Golf course designers Robert Trent Jones, Joe Lee, Dick Wilson and a number of Fazios have left an indelible imprint on Caribbean golf, and with so many Florida golf courses and beaches as crowded as they are, vacationers are branching out, past the Bahamas, into the relative solitude of the islands.

That's not to say that there are no *slow* rounds of golf in the Caribbean. Many potential golfers play their first round ever on vacation, and while we applaud their enthusiasm and dedication, that's not always the group I want to get behind. Play early in the day, or late, or both, and leave the mid-day sun and the backups on the par-threes to those who haven't yet experienced them.

Be prepared for "island rules," both on the course and off. On the course, if the local rule is "drop one where it went out and add a stroke," by all means drop one, add one and get on with it. Unless you intend to play your way into Q-School you'll be wasting your time and everyone else's foraging in the tangle of hibiscus and bouganvillea vines which often line the fairways. Island rules also dictate that there is no such thing as a straight putt—now matter how straight it may look—since everything "breaks toward the water"...and you *are* on an island.

But the most important golfing rule is: Pay Attention to Your Caddy. A fair guess is that fully 90 percent of the caddies I've worked with in

the islands are five-handicaps or less. These young men will be playing this same course within a few hours of your departure, just as they do nearly every day of the week. They know these courses backward and forward, and if they say hit a five-iron where at home you would hit a seven, hit the five. You're not back home. The gentle breeze you feel in the middle of the fairway is usually gale force at the peninsula green. Always, always hit more club. I've been wading in the surf around many a seaside green in my day, and I've never found a single ball *behind* the putting surface.

Off-the-course island rules dictate that if you intend to have dinner at 8 p.m. you book your reservation for seven. A few cocktails and a little conversation is appropriate anyway, so the time between placing your order and its arrival will be time well spent. Don't ever give your cab driver directions, even if you've visited before, or even if you've lived there all your life. Give him or her only the address, then sit back and relax. If you haven't arrived in an hour or so, bring it up, politely.

The preeminent island rule is: Call Your Travel Agent...First. Decide where you want to go and when (or let them help), then let your travel agency do the legwork. You'll get the best dates, the best rates and the most direct route. All you have to do is show up.

Sandy Lane Hotel & Golf Club

WHEN RONALD TREE RETIRED AS A member of the British Parliament, he decided to create a tropical retreat where his guests could enjoy "an elegant country house party in the English tradition." After the Second World War he acquired a sugar plantation in Barbados named Sandy Lane, and in 1959 began construction of the hotel's 48 original rooms. It was an immediate success. Vacationers from the Continent flocked to Tree's "country house," and Sandy Lane topped the list of Caribbean haunts for the affluent European traveler.

Nearly 30 years in the salt air of the Caribbean will erode any facility, no matter how well it is maintained, so in 1991 the hotel closed for six months and was renovated and refurbished from top to bottom. The results are stunning. Sandy Lane's luxurious image has always been cornerstoned by its Palladian architecture, carved from honey-colored coral and crafted with meticulous detail. That detail was maintained and enhanced during the renovation, and the new Sandy Lane is even more striking (if that's possible) than the old.

Sandy Lane is also the site of Barbados' only 18-hole championship-caliber golf course, a par-72, 6,600-yard affair that plays adjacent to the ocean and through the rolling hills surrounding the resort. On these hillsides sit some of the most luxurious and imaginatively designed mansions in the Caribbean (President Ronald Reagan frolicked in the surf just below one of these during his term in office). The fairways are well groomed and fairly wide open, and the hotel renovation included a new irrigation system to keep them in top condition year round.

The putting surfaces are impeccable, but though they roll true they are more affected by the "break toward the water" credo than many others in the islands. I'm not sure why that is, but I am sure that the caddies know these greens like the backs of their hands, and if they say "six inches outside right," putt it six inches outside right. Sandy Lane boasts one of the most friendly and knowledgable caddy staffs in the Caribbean, and I'm sure I shot at least six strokes better (I've carded two 81s and a 79 there) than I would have on my own.

A featured attraction of golf at Sandy Lane is the unlimited free play for hotel guests, representing a savings of over $450 during a seven-night stay. Playing the course is a delight; playing it for free is a perk of immense proportion.

Although the resort prides itself on its casual, relaxed atmosphere, Wednesday and Saturday nights during high season are formal, an opportunity to break out the tuxedos and evening dresses and really do it up. And the courteous, efficient service staff shines even more brightly for these occasions.

Daytime activities include tennis, watersports from windsurfing to waterskiing, and cycling to nearby Bridgetown, the island's capital city. There are so many things to occupy your time in this tropical paradise it's no wonder Sandy Lane has been the vacation destination for such luminaries as Queen Elizabeth and Lord and Lady Astor. But you don't have to be royalty to be treated that way at Sandy Lane. You just have to be here. ■

Sandy Lane Hotel & Golf Club
St. James, Barbados
West Indies

LOCATION: 30 minutes from Grantley Adams Airport, nine miles from Bridgetown.

ACCOMMODATIONS: 91 double rooms and 30 suites, most overlooking the ocean.

DINING/ENTERTAINMENT: Sandy Bay Restaurant, overlooking the ocean serving Bajan specialties and fine French cuisine; The Seashell Restaurant, open during high season offering Italian fare nightly except Fridays; five bars and lounges serving refreshments and cocktails and featuring nightly entertainment; 24-hour room service.

AMENITIES: 18-hole golf course (green fees included in room rate); five tennis courts (two lighted); 3,000-square-foot free-form swimming pool; complimentary watersports including Hobie Cat and sunfish sailing, snorkeling, waterskiing and windsurfing.

RATES: Begin at $1,060 for 4-day/3-night golf vacation (green fee included) and $2,080 for 8-days/7-nights.

RESERVATIONS: Call (809) 432-1311.

Casa de Campo

Setting the standard for world-class resorts

THERE ARE MORE THAN A FEW golfers, amateur and professional alike, who hope to someday meet Pete Dye in person. Many would use the opportunity to probe the mind of the world-renowned golf course architect to gain a better understanding of what design philosophy goes into the creation of some of the better known Dye layouts like Harbour Town Golf Links, PGA West, etc.

Some, including me (and perhaps tour pro Mark Calcavecchia, who stumbled badly on the Dye-designed Ocean Course at Kiawah Island, S.C., during the 1991 Ryder Cup matches), would use the opportunity to force-feed Mr. Dye a few of the railroad ties—a Dye design trademark—they've been forced to play around, across and out from under these many years.

Thus are the trappings of genius. There is no gray area involved in Dye-designed golf courses; it's black and white—you either love them or hate them—and the feeling carries over to the man responsible.

But no golfer we're aware of has anything but high praise for Dye's masterpiece in the Caribbean, The Teeth of the Dog course at Casa de Campo in La Romana in the Dominican Republic. The Teeth of the Dog (the name given to the sharp, teeth-like coral reefs along the coast of Hispaniola) opened for play in 1971, and has perenially been ranked among the top 100 courses by nearly every major golf publication ever since. Director of golf Gilles Gagnon has said that "if you take away The Teeth of the Dog, we're just another golf resort," even though Casa's other two Dye-designed courses—The Links and La Romana—also have garnered rave reviews since they opened in 1976 and 1989, respectively. The love/hate relationship apparently begins at home.

Located on the sun-drenched southeastern coast of the Dominican Republic, Casa de Campo offers 7,000 acres of the finest in Latin American resort living with a distinctly international flavor, and has achieved the status of one of the world's finest and most complete recreational retreats.

In addition to the great golf, Casa features 13 clay tennis courts (10 lighted), polo on two playing fields and two practice facilities, an equestrian center with a dude ranch and a rodeo arena, all the water sports you can imagine with three white-sand beaches, 19 swimming pools and a full-service marina, and the renowned Shooting Centre, 150 acres of the most extensive facilities in the world, with sporting clays and Olympic-caliber trap, skeet and flyer shooting.

Casa de Campo also boasts 11 restaurants and lounges including the Lago Grill and La Piazzetta, a romantic Italian setting with a strolling violinist.

But golf is the real attraction here, and that means The Teeth, whose eight seaside holes (which are routed north-and-south so the Caribbean Sea is always a distraction) and 10 inland holes abound with a unique assortment of pot bunkers, strategically designed greens set against ocean backdrops and hand-sculpted putting surfaces....and no railroad ties!

No matter how you feel about Dye, The Teeth of the Dog is inarguably one of the finest courses in the Caribbean, and in the world. I hope that if I have the chance to meet him in person, that's the first thing that comes to mind. ■

CASA DE CAMPO - LA ROMANA, DOMINICAN REPUBLIC

LOCATION: Dominican Republic, on the island of Hispaniola, reached by air from San Juan via American Airlines or charter.

ACCOMMODATIONS: 950 guest rooms including 268 casitas, two-, three- and four-bedroom villas, and the Premier Club.

DINING/ENTERTAINMENT: Eleven restaurants and lounges including Lago Grill, open-air facility overlooking the golf course; Tropicana, fresh local seafood; Casa Del Rio, fine gourmet cuisine with a breathtaking view of the Chavon River; Cafe Del Sol.

AMENITIES: 54 holes of golf (Pete Dye); polo; Shooting Centre; Equestrian Centre; 13 tennis courts; water sport facilities including 19 swimming pools, marina; fitness center.

RATES: 4 day/3 night packages available from approx. $600 to $1,000.

RESERVATIONS: Call (800) 8-PREMIER.

Half Moon Club

First-class golf at a world-class resort

IT'S BEEN SAID THAT ONE MEASURE of a truly great resort may be taken in the tenure of its staff. If that's so, then the Half Moon Club in Montego Bay, Jamaica must surely be one of the finest, since its general manager, Heinz Simonitsch, has been on the job for over a quarter of a century. Coincidentally, many of his employees have been right along with him the entire time.

To be honest, if I'd known more about Half Moon during the past 25 years I probably would have been there, too. This perennial AAA Four-Diamond award winner has been called "one of the finest resort hotels anywhere in the world" by noted travel writer Rene Lecler, author of *The Three Hundred Best Hotels in the World*, who also says that the crescent-shaped beach from which the resort derives its name is "the Caribbean at its best." This is the kind of resort that makes you want to sell your house, pack only your most important possessions (at Half Moon those would be your golf clubs, your bathing suit and your evening wear) and stick the kids and the dogs—okay, not the dogs—in boarding school. It's impossible to *not* have a great time here. Heck, they're already having a great time; all you need to do is show up.

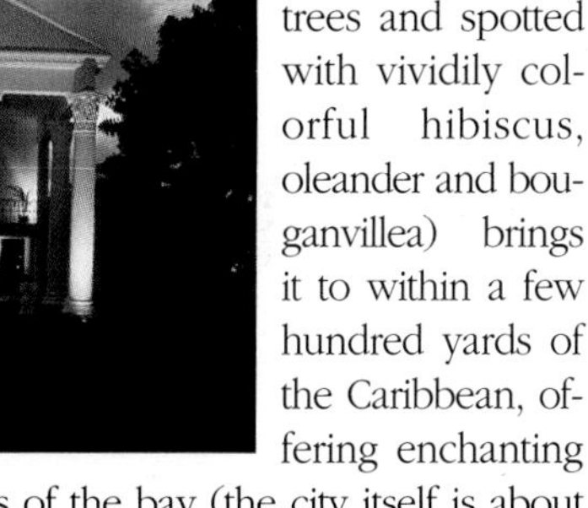

As well as being a first-class hotel, Half Moon offers top-notch golf, as in Robert Trent Jones Sr., who designed the Half Moon Golf Club in 1961. The routing of the 7,125-yard course, (lined with palm trees and spotted with vividily colorful hibiscus, oleander and bouganvillea) brings it to within a few hundred yards of the Caribbean, offering enchanting views of the bay (the city itself is about six miles west) and the stunning hotel property.

Length and wind are the "extenuating circumstances" on this course—oddly (for the Caribbean, that is) water is in play on only seven holes. But when it's in play, it's *really* in play. No. 4, for example, looks to be a straightaway par-four of 381 yards. *No problem.* Until you notice *(breathe in)* that from the tee you can't see the green because the hole's not really straight at all and that it's a dogleg left where the second shot must play over the water that fronts the putting surface and no matter how far you smash your drive and how far to the right you keep it you're still probably going to have to snap-hook a short iron to reach the green in regulation and the only time I ever "drew" a short iron in my life was when my pitching wedge once struck a tree root before making contact with the ball and I was trying to fade the shot anyway *(breathe out).*

So? You have to make at least one bogey per round to keep your perspective, don't you?

This is not by any means Trent Jones at his *unrelenting* best. Courses such as Congressional in Bethesda, Md., and Firestone in Akron, Ohio, win that prize hands down. Instead, Jones sprinkled in a few holes that reward the resort player if he or she is thinking clearly that day. As in many instances in the Caribbean, position is usually preferable to distance. However, if I play the 446-yard, par-4 sixth hole or the collossal 462-yard, par-four ninth just once more the way I have in the past (more double bogies than I care to admit) I may be forced to rethink my position.

The inward nine, while slightly shorter than the outward, has a few holes—15 and 16, in particular—that could reasonably be deemed malevolent. Fifteen is another goodly sized par-four (385

Below: The mile-long, crescent shaped beach from which Half Moon derives its name. Above right: Superior accommodations are a hallmark.

yards) where the second shot must carry water that fronts the green and runs further away from the putting surface on the right to closer in on the left, which is also the way the green is positioned. The difficulty of the hole is determined that morning when the hole is cut in the green: The right side is good; the left is bad...very bad.

No. 16, a par-three of 176 yards, also has water enroute, although it is equidistant from tee and green and should be a non-factor if, as I said, you're thinking clearly. Lose concentration for a moment, though, and you'll be fishing your ball from the stream or digging it (ofttimes repeatedly) out of one of the three greenside bunkers. *No problem.*

For all its opulence, Half Moon is relaxed—to the max. Other than "formal night" on Saturday (that's why you'll want to pack your evening wear) preferred dress is extremely casual in the evenings and bathing suit and coverup during the day. (I was there for about five days before I wore anything below the knee.) All three meals are served in the elegant Sea Grape Terrace restaurant, and for a special treat the Sugar Mill, overlooking the golf course, serves some of the tastiest and spiciest Jamaican cuisine in all of Montego Bay.

The concierge staff will be happy to arrange sightseeing trips to such famous attractions as Dunn's River Falls in Ocho Rios or rafting trips on the Martha Brae river....if you decide to leave the property, that is. After all, Heinz Simonitsch has devoted 25 years of his life to making Half Moon one of the finest resorts in the world. It would be downright unneighborly to not take full advantage of his hospitality. ■

HALF MOON CLUB — MONTEGO BAY, JAMAICA

LOCATION: P.O. Box 80, Montego Bay, Jamaica, West Indies; six miles east of Sangster International Airport.

ACCOMMODATIONS: 89 deluxe rooms, 78 suites and 36 villas.

DINING/ENTERTAINMENT: Seagrape Terrace, breakfast, lunch, dinner, beachside setting; The Sugar Mill, world-famous cuisine overlooking the golf course; The Cedar Bar, cocktail service from 10 a.m., nightly entertainment.

AMENITIES: 18 holes of golf; 13 tennis courts (seven lighted); 17 swimming pools; cycling; all water sports including snorkeling, scuba, windsurfing and waterskiing; squash.

MEETING FACILITIES: 12,000 square feet (six rooms) accommodating up to 350; full-service audio/visual department.

RATES: Vary by season, from $120 - $660.

RESERVATIONS: Call (809) 953-2615.

Tryall Golf, Tennis & Beach Club

I'VE USED THE WORD "STUNNING" in this book too many times to dredge it up again; I'd hate for you to think I'm suffering the dreaded Chicken Little syndrome. So I won't use the "S" word to describe the villas at Tryall, 30 minutes west of Montego Bay. But I will tell you that my stay in those villas was the first time in my life I'd had a cook, chambermaid, laundress and gardener as part of the amenities package at a golf resort, and that the accommodations were so.... *you know*....they warranted the additional attention.

You're probably already familiar with the Tryall golf course, it having been the site of the Johnnie Walker World Championship won by Fred Couples at the beginning of his 1991-1992 "streak." Some of the tournament video work showed off the lodgings, but they were short clips, bites really, that didn't (couldn't) deliver the impact these private residences for rent have in person.

Naturally, you will pay dearly for a week or two in such luxury, but if there is such a thing as a "once in a lifetime" vacation, this most assuredly is it.

The resort also features 52 rooms in the Tryall Great House, built in 1834, and they are spacious, tastefully decorated in island colors and fabrics and much, much more than adequate. The facility also comprises the Great House Restaurant, which serves breakfast and dinner daily—lunch is served at the Great House Pool. During high season the Beach Bar serves Continental breakfast, lunch and an informal dinner (lunch only the rest of the year).

This beautiful 2,200-acre plantation only 14 miles from Montego Bay offers an endless array of activities like swimming at the resort's private beach or in the oversized fresh-water pool, watersports such as snorkeling, sunfish sailing, windsurfing and pedal boats, deep-sea fishing (by arrangement), tennis on nine Laykold courts (five lighted) and spectator sports including horseracing, polo, soccer and cricket.

The premier attraction is the Tryall golf course, an 18-hole, par-71 layout designed by course architect Ralph Plummer. Cutting through the valleys and along the rolling hillsides, it plays to a moderate 6,680 yards, though many of those yards, it seems, are uphill. During the off season (April 15 to Dec. 14) there is no charge to hotel guests for golf privileges. In high season you can expect to pay about $50 per day or $300 per week.

You'll find your driver is of little use here, as most of the fairways require position rather than length, but the putting surfaces are large enough to hold slightly mis-hit approaches and true enough to frequently give you a chance at birdie. It's a thoroughly enjoyable experience, in keeping with the rest of the resort's amenities. If this isn't the vacation of *your* lifetime, you travel in completely different circles than I. ■

For information call (809) 952-5110.

Jamaica Jamaica Resort

TO BE QUITE FRANK, WHEN I THINK of the finest accommodations in Jamaica, the Jamaica Jamaica Resort at Runaway Bay is not the first place that comes to mind. There's absolutely nothing wrong with them, mind you. Actually, though some rooms are rather small they have recently been renovated, and they do offer everything you need to make your stay a very pleasant one. But they certainly don't compare to the villas at Half Moon or Tryall, or to a few of the other SuperClub properties on the island such as Boscobel Beach, Hedonism II and the ultra-exclusive Grand Lido.

So what? Jamaica Jamaica isn't *about* accommodations. Trust me, you won't be using your room for anything other than a place to shower and sleep. At Jamaica Jamaica, the conga line forms shortly after breakfast, and once you attach yourself to it you'll need radical surgery to get disconnected.

This is the most fun you can have standing up, sitting down or in the prone position (especially lounging on the private clothing-optional beach). A "sports enthusiast's and beach lover's dream" is the way it's described in the brochure, and for once it's apparent that not all

public relations people were lawyers in a past life.

SuperClubs owns and operates its own golf club, Runaway Bay, a par-72 seaside delight adjacent to the resort that lets you determine how to play its holes, instead of the other way around. The course comprises surprisingly few water hazards, and by and large the fairways are wide and the greens receptive to a variety of approach shots. A nice additional touch is the complimentary Golf Academy—remember, SuperClub resorts are all-inclusive, so everything from food and drink to trips and transfers are paid for up front—which features video presentations, swing analysis, semi-private and private instruction and tournaments.

Outdoor activities at the resort include snorkeling, scuba (with certification), sailing or cruising, tennis on four lighted courts, horseback riding, etc. The to-do list is virtually endless. Or you can break up a day or two with side trips to nearby Ocho Rios or scenic Dunns River Falls.

Three meals a day are served buffet style on the Beach Terrace near the pool, but evening dining offers the option of an intimate gourmet restaurant serving island specialties and Continental cuisine, and featuring a wine list that ranks with the best on the island.

For evening entertainment there's the piano bar in the lobby area, and a reggae/rock band is featured nightly. There's also the Jamaica Jamaica Disco, a wall of impenetrable sound that doesn't abate until the wee hours. Then it's back to your room for a few hours sleep, a change of clothes....and the whole thing begins again.

I promise you, your accommodations will be the *last* thing you'll remember about Jamaica Jamaica. ■

Jamaica Jamaica
Runaway Bay, Jamaica

LOCATION: Approximately one hour from Sangster International Airport in Montego Bay.

ACCOMMODATIONS: 238 guest rooms including four deluxe suites.

DINING/ENTERTAINMENT: Three meals a day are served at the buffet-style Beach Terrace near the main swimming pool; additionally, an intimate gourmet restaurant serves a la carte island specialties and fine Continental cuisine in a casual atmosphere.

AMENITIES: 18-hole golf course; four tennis courts (lighted); swimming pool; open-air fitness center; complete watersports center offering snorkeling, kayaking, windsurfing, sunfish sailing and scuba with certification; Nautilus gym with free weights; three Jacuzzis; horseback riding; volleyball; exercise and aerobics classes; croquet; cricket and soccer lessons; complimentary golf school; indoor game room.

RATES: 4-days/3-nights from $502 for a standard room to $754 for a beachfront suite.

RESERVATIONS: Call (800) 859-SUPER.

Wyndham Rose Hall

WYNDHAM HOTELS & RESORTS IS well known across the U.S. and throughout the Caribbean for its luxurious accommodations, its wealth of amenities and its meeting and conference facilities. But even corporate headquarters would admit they've hit the jackpot with their Wyndham Rose Hall resort just east of "downtown" Montego Bay. Sited on 400 acres of sugar plantation along a 1,000-foot stretch of secluded beachfront, Rose Hall has more meeting space than any other resort on the island, and draws heavily on the conference and convention business from the states.

But regular resort guests (that's us) are not lost in the shuffle here; indeed, Wyndham's personalized service doesn't "trickle down" to individual travelers, it begins with them.

Wyndham Rose Hall features 500 recently renovated and redecorated guest rooms, with 26 suites that are among the most elegant in Jamaica. All rooms and suites offer ocean or mountain views, and all are equipped with private balconies, satellite TV and all the little extras that bridge the gap between good hotels and great hotels.

Great hotels, of course, have great sur-

roundings, and Rose Hall certainly qualifies, backing up as it does from the beach into the foothills of Jamaica's Blue Mountains, where the finest coffee beans in the world (and the most expensive) are grown. And from this centralized location you're only minutes from some of the island's featured attractions such as the Rose Hall Great House, rafting on the Martha Brae River, the stunning beaches of Negril, and Dunns River Falls, the most photographed waterfall in the islands.

But Wyndham Rose Hall is another of those special places you'll find difficult to leave. Besides the 18-hole golf course—with fairways bordered by jagged mountain cliffs, holes that play down lush grassy plateaus, putting surfaces that sit directly adjacent to 30-foot waterfalls and a peninsula green surrounded by the world's largest water hazard (the Caribbean Sea)—there is tennis on seven lighted courts, a large free-form pool with swim-up bar, an open-air fitness center (with aerobics) and a watersports facility with scuba, snorkeling, windsurfing and sailing.

You'll also find fine dining at Rose Hall at The Verandah, which features Continental and Caribbean specialties in a tropically elegant atmosphere, or at Ambrosia, the restaurant at the Country Club that offers Italian cuisine in a very private setting.

Nightlife at the resort is *no problem,* with entertainment in the Terrace Restaurant and music videos and high energy in the Junkanoo Nightclub.

Truly, every conceivable diversion under the sun (and moon) can be found at Wyndham Rose Hall, and it's a wonder those conference attendees get any real work done. How do you find one of those jobs, anyway? ■

Wyndham Rose Hall
Montego Bay, Jamaica

LOCATION: 10 minutes east of Sangster International Airport.

ACCOMMODATIONS: 500 guest rooms including 26 deluxe suites.

DINING/ENTERTAINMENT: Brasserie, casual for breakfast, lunch and dinner; The Terrace Restaurant, indoor/outdoor dining with nightly entertainment; The Verandah, dining with an international flair; Ambrosia, serving Italian fare; The Pool Grille, refreshments and snacks; Junkanoo Nightclub; Gazebo Bar; in-pool bar.

AMENITIES: 18-hole golf course; seven tennis courts (lighted); swimming pool with swim-up bar; open-air fitness center; complete watersports center offering snorkeling, windsurfing, sunfish, sailboats and scuba trips; horseback riding nearby.

MEETING FACILITIES: 11,000 square feet including 7,500-square-foot ballroom.

RATES: From $110 to $750.

RESERVATIONS: Call (800) 822-4200.

Hyatt Regency Cerromar & Hyatt Dorado Beach:
mainstays of classic Caribbean golf

Hyatt Dorado Beach

LOCATION: 22 miles west of San Juan on the north coast of Puerto Rico.

ACCOMMODATIONS: 300 rooms in 16 adjacent buildings offering poolview, oceanview, golfview rooms and fairway estates.

DINING/ENTERTAINMENT: Surf Room, Caribbean, Continental and local dishes for dinner in a dramatic setting; Ocean Terrace, breakfast, lunch and dinner with nightly theme parties; Su Casa Restaurant, traditional Spanish and Caribbean cuisine in an authentic Spanish hacienda dating to 1900; lobby bar and additional lounges spread throughout the property.

AMENITIES: 36 holes of golf (Robert Trent Jones); seven all-weather tennis courts (lighted) under the direction of Peter Burwash International; 25-meter swimming pool, lap pool; water sports including windsurfing, waterskiing, deep-sea fishing and snorkeling; children's activities program; movies; bicycling; indoor/outdoor games; excursions to Old San Juan and other points of interest.

MEETING FACILITIES: Costa Del Mar meeting center comprises a 6,000-square-foot divisible ballroom and a 2,000-square-foot prefunction area and boardroom for up to 16 people; Salon del Mar, overlooking the ocean for groups to 225.

RATES: Golf packages in all four seasons are available. Call for rates.

RESERVATIONS: Call (800) 233-1234 or (809) 796-1234.

FOR MORE THAN 30 YEARS THE Dorado Beach (it wasn't a Hyatt until 1985) has been serving up its special brand of Caribbean ambience—casual yet elegant, relaxed yet vibrant, with a distinctly Caribbean nature yet with decidedly Old World Spanish character. Those have been the featured attractions since the late 1950s and the days of Laurence Rockefeller, and they remain today at the Hyatt Dorado Beach and the Hyatt Regency Cerromar Beach, sister resorts on the north coast of Puerto Rico 22 miles from San Juan.

As you're well aware, Robert Trent Jones played no small part in the development of the Caribbean in general as a

Trent Jones' North and South courses are adjacent to the Hyatt Regency Cerromar and the Atlantic.

true golf destination, as his substantial contributions to the Dorado and Cerromar properties bear witness. The original course at Dorado was once what is now the two back nines of the East and West courses (North and South are at Cerromar a few miles away). The 7,005-yard East is the site each fall of the Mazda Champions and features pool-sized, moderately undulating putting surfaces and the opportunity to get your ball wet, often. It also offers views of the ocean from many of its tees and greens, and is widely considered the more scenic of the four.

West, at 6,913 yards, has many such similar vistas, and tee to green there isn't a more beautiful golf hole than the 185-yard, par-three 13th, sited on a spit of land that juts into the Atlantic.

Hyatt Regency Cerromar Beach

LOCATION: 22 miles west of San Juan on the north coast of Puerto Rico.

ACCOMMODATIONS: 504 guest rooms including 19 suites; most rooms offer ocean views and private balconies.

DINING/ENTERTAINMENT: Medici's, Northern Italian specialties (including antipasto bar) in spacious, open atmosphere; Costa de Oro, steak house-style menu; Swan Cafe, three-level restaurant for breakfast and lunch at the edge of a lake; Flamingo Bar, cocktails overlooking the River Pool and Atlantic; El Coqui, sports bar.

AMENITIES: 36 holes of golf (Robert Trent Jones); 14 all-weather tennis courts under the direction of Peter Burwash International; River Pool (4.5 acres), world's longest fresh-water swimming pool (five connected free-form pools) with 14 waterfalls, subterranean Jacuzzi, waterslides, children's pool, walks and bridges; all water sports including wind-surfing, waterskiing, deep-sea fishing and snorkeling; children's activities program; movies; bicycling; indoor/outdoor games; excursions to Old San Juan and other points of interest.

MEETING FACILITIES: Flexible function space for up to 1,700 people including 11 conference rooms and Foyer Grande, with space for up to 50 exhibit booths.

RATES: Golf packages in all four seasons are available. Call for rates.

RESERVATIONS: Call (800) 233-1234 or (809) 796-1234.

The North and South courses are equally as long (6,841 yards and 7,047 yards, respectively) and equally as scenic. Water is in play on the South course on 14 holes, however—including the entire inward nine—and when added to the courses length these hazards are at times nearly impossible to overcome.

But most of the fresh water on the island, it seems, is in Cerromar's 4-1/2-acre River Pool, a 1,776-yard (526-feet longer than the Empire State Building) water playground that pumps over 22,000 gallons of water per minute downstream. Floating from one end to the other takes an astounding 15 minutes through its 14 waterfalls, a subterranean Jacuzzi, tropical landscaping and waterslides.

Other amenities at both Cerromar and Dorado include tennis from Peter Burwash Internation on all-weather, lighted courts, the *usual* (I use the word reluctantly) watersports, including waterskiing, scuba, snorkeling and deep-sea fishing, and excursions to some of the area attractions like Old San Juan and—my favorite "side trip" in the Caribbean—El Yunque, the 28,000-acre tropical rain forest, to the best of my knowledge the only one in the U.S. Rainfall here is measured in yards, not inches, and it's fascinating to be in almost total darkness under the jungle canopy in the middle of a bright, sunny day. I highly recommend this adventure, which will happily be arranged by the concierge in either hotel.

Trent Jones golf, superior accommodations, fantastic food in a myriad of restaurants, casinos, nightlife galore, sun, sand, surf...Wait a minute. I think I'm beginning to feel the Hyatt Touch. ■

Palmas del Mar

Old World elegance on Puerto Rico's southeast coast

THE PALMAS DEL MAR RESORT ON the Caribbean side of Puerto Rico bills itself as "the new American Riviera." That may in fact be the case, but since I'm not really sure where the old American Riviera was, and I've never been to *the* Riviera, well...

In any case, Palmas del Mar's 2,700 acres of rolling hillsides and tropical beachfront offer the finest in Caribbean resort living in 102 rooms in the Candelero Hotel, 195 villas overlooking the beach, harbor or golf course, and especially in (my personal favorite) the 23-suite European-style Palmas Inn. The Inn is a secluded guest residence with a private swimming pool, nightly cocktail parties and views of the Caribbean Sea from every room. Its tastefully furnished room interiors evoke the charm of a small Mediterranean hotel, and the service staff is well versed in the art of gracious hospitality.

But the villas have their strong points, too, such as full kitchens (although with 11 restaurants on property it's doubtful you'll be spending much time hovering over a stove), fairway views and the option of up to three-bedrooms. The Candelero Hotel is just large enough to offer every conceivable amenity and service, and just small enough to offer

them with a decidedly personal touch.

The 6,690-yard Gary Player-designed golf course has its share of sand and water hazards, but the most hazardous distractions are the vistas of the Caribbean from nearly every hole. The tiny (140-yard) par-3 third hole, for example, should be an 8-iron, a putt and out, but it runs directly adjacent to the white-sand, never-ending Palmas beach, and between the devilish sea breezes and the very latest in "miniaturized" swimwear parading by, you'll be lucky to card double-bogey.

Palmas offers fine dining and nightlife aplenty in the Candelero Lobby Bar and the Galeria Club, an intimate lounge featuring soft rock, jazz and island sounds. But the most fun you can have at night (unless your home course is lighted) is to be found in the intimate little casino next to the Palmas Inn, which holds only a dozen or so gaming tables and 50 slot machines. It was there I learned the game of roulette, and then gave back everything I'd "earned" that evening at the blackjack tables, plus a little more. That's the way they do it on the Riviera, right? ■

Horseback rides in the surf are available from Palmas del Mar's new 42-horse equestrian center.

PALMAS DEL MAR RESORT - HUMACAO, PUERTO RICO

LOCATION: P.O. Box 2020, Humacao, Puerto Rico 00661; one-hour drive from San Juan Airport.

ACCOMMODATIONS: 320 guest rooms, suites and one- to three-bedroom villas.

DINING/ENTERTAINMENT: Eleven restaurants and lounges including Las Garzas, facing pool and patio serving Continental, American and Puerto Rican fare; Azzurro, northern Italian cuisine in an elegant setting; Cafe de la Plaza, Puerto Rican specialties; Le Bistroquet; La Maison Francaise; Galeria Club.

AMENITIES: 18 holes of golf; 20 tennis courts; seven swimming pools; equestrain center; complete water sport facilities, marina; fitness center; 3-1/2-mile beach; casino; pro shops; gift shops; boutiques.

RATES: Call for rates and packages.

RESERVATIONS: Call (800) 221-4874.

Four Seasons Resort Nevis

A new resort lives up to the old Four Seasons standards

I'VE ALWAYS HAD THE UTMOST respect for Christopher Columbus, not only for his accomplishments, which were formidable, but also for his initiative, his determination and his daring. But there is one other truly worthy of the same admiration—adulation, actually—and that is Columbus' travel agent. Think about it: This agent managed to get Columbus, an Italian gentleman, on a Portugese ship, using borrowed Spanish money, for his first Caribbean cruise. An achievement like that would be recognized today by the American Society of Travel Agents with chicken Kiev for 200 at an awards dinner and an engraved plaque. Even better, this first cruise took Chris to such exotic destinations as the Bahamas, Jamaica and Nevis in the West Indies. Why, if it weren't for the incredibly lengthy travel time and all those burdensome layovers, and totally disregarding the fact that the agent thought he pointed Columbus toward Cathay and not the Caribbean, he or she would at this moment be in the ASTA hall of fame.

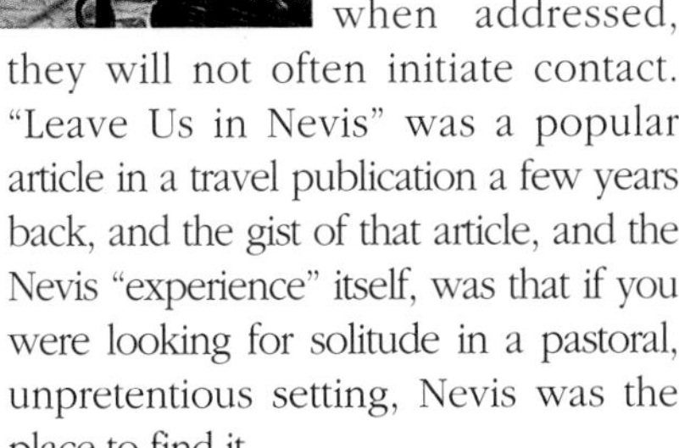

While most people are aware of the goings on in the Bahamas and Jamaica, in Nevis things remained much the same for the next five centuries. Sort of. Of course, the trappings of civilization were always in place, on pace with the rest of the Caribbean, but in Nevis there remained a certain detachment from the outside world. Nevisians were and are somewhat aloof. The "no problem" spirit of the residents is quite evident, but they don't even bother to mouth the words—it is assumed. The island is virtually drug free, and while islanders are very friendly when addressed, they will not often initiate contact. "Leave Us in Nevis" was a popular article in a travel publication a few years back, and the gist of that article, and the Nevis "experience" itself, was that if you were looking for solitude in a pastoral, unpretentious setting, Nevis was the place to find it.

So there was apprehension on the part of many when Four Seasons Hotels and Resorts announced a few years back that they would begin building a 196-room resort and golf course along Pinney's Beach, a 2,000-foot stretch of white-sanded, palm tree-lined heaven in the shadow of Nevis Peak. Some islanders were worried that the resort would change the character of Nevis, opening it to the distractions and diversions and discombobulations of the "outside." Frequent visitors—an increasing number of which were coming from the U.S.—were worried that the complexion of the island, a safe haven to be enjoyed in near total privacy, would forever be lost. And whether they admit it or not, Four Seasons management had to be somewhat on edge: What if you build it, and they *don't* come? Nevis is not a particularly easy island to reach, although the resort has gone to great lengths to lighten the load. And since many golfers still believe that even established Caribbean courses are substandard, there had to be a feeling that it would be some time before the course would mature.

Not to worry. The resultant Four Seasons Resort Nevis has pleased most everyone. Residents for the most part regard the property as unobtrusive (many think it a welcome addition), plus the resort employs nearly 400 of them, making it even more palatable. Island visitors, who have for years walked or driven by Pinney's Beach, can barely tell the structures are in place, so finely

The 445-yard par-four 18th hole at Nevis plays into the prevailing wind, out to the Caribbean Sea.

tuned are they to their surroundings. And even though Four Seasons had no intention originally of marketing the resort as a "golf" destination, an astounding 35 percent of first-year, first-time guests playing the golf course gave them pause for reflection.

There's no real cause for amazement when it comes to the course, however. The Robert Trent Jones Jr. design stretches some 6,766 yards from the tips, winding around the foothills of 3,500-foot Nevis Peak, through its valleys, across huge ravines layered in dense jungle vegetation, and finishing at the spectacular 445-yard, par-four 18th on the Caribbean Sea. Along the way are the testy but playable par-threes—the 230-yard 14th is a bit more testy than it is playable—medium to long par-fours, and an award-winning set of par-fives, including the mammoth, 663-yard 15th, which features a 240-yard jungle carry from the back tees.

Although open only a year, the course, as does the resort, plays "older." Nevis experienced a drought of some proportion a few years back, but the water table has since returned to normal, and the again-frequent afternoon rain showers and 10 or 11 hours of daily sunshine, along with 78- to 82-degree average temperatures, provide Nevis with a growing season that seems to exceed the alloted 12 months.

"Lush" is certainly an understatement here, and the natural beauty of the place demanded guest quarters of equal measure. The rooms and suites at Four Seasons Resort Nevis now are among the largest and most elegant in the Caribbean. Sited in 12 two-story guest

Four Seasons Resort Nevis, West Indies

LOCATION: On the leeward side of the island; approximately a two-hour flight southeast of Miami.

ACCOMMODATIONS: 196 rooms and suites, from 550 to 2,200 square feet, all with oversized private verandah.

DINING/ENTERTAINMENT: The Dining Room, tropical elegance in open-air setting serving sefood, steaks and lobster for dinner only—complete wine list; the Grill Room, casual, with breakfast and lunch buffets; the Ocean Terrace, noon to midnight beverage service, live entertainment; the Library, intimate room for reading and relaxing with beverage service 4 p.m. to midnight; the Tap Room, entertainment lounge with stage; the Pool Pavilion, light fare and beverages.

AMENITIES: 18 holes of golf (Robert Trent Jones Jr.); 10 all-weather and clay tennis courts, operated by Peter Burwash International; large free-form swimming pool; water sports including windsurfing, water-skiing, deep-sea fishing and snorkeling; a complimentary children's activities program, "Kids for All Seasons;" volleyball; croquet; health club with sauna, whirlpool, massage and beauty salon.

MEETING FACILITIES: More than 5,000 square feet of space, including a divisible ballroom accommodating up to 300.

RATES: Deluxe rooms from $225 to $459; suites from $425 to $2,900.

RESERVATIONS: Call (800) 332-3442; in Canada (800) 268-6282, or (809) 469-1111.

cottages—10 of which open directly to the beach; the other two face Nevis Peak and the golf course—which are central to the West Indies plantation-style Great House, the accommodations feature twice-daily maid service, concealed remote-controlled television and VCR, an honor bar and exceptionally large baths with double vanities, hairdryers, cotton robes, tubs and separate showers. Executive suites have large bedrooms separated from the living room by glass doors, providing extra space and privacy, and there are seven distinctive ocean and luxury suites with up to three bedrooms and enormous verandahs for private outdoor dining or relaxing.

Naturally, you'll pay for the luxury—from $225 for a deluxe golf-view room in the off-season, to $2,900 for a three-bedroom suite in high-season—and meal plans are a bit pricey, too, since most of the staples are imported. But if you're prepared to pay the tariff, the vacation you receive for your money is well worth the cost. In fact, the cuisine at the Four Seasons is alone almost worth the price of admission. The Grill Room serves breakfast, lunch and dinner daily in an open-air setting enhanced by its brightly colored tile and even more brightly colored floral arrangements. The breakfast buffet features such specialties as Grenadian spice muffins and Caribbean hot cross buns, tropical fruits and juices, and standards like omelettes and grilled meats. The lunch buffet has an equally outstanding assortment of salads and appetizers, such as the curried breadfruit with chicken or the gingered pork. Dinner in the Grill Room is very nice, with steaks and chops, lamb or even local range hen.

But you must, absolutely must, have dinner in the Dining Room at least every other night. Located on the second floor of the Great House, the Dining Room is an elegantly islandish Four Seasons restaurant, and that means the cuisine is phenomenal. The surroundings of planked floors and open-rafter ceilings with fans and a cut-stone fireplace set the occasion up perfectly, but the food is the headliner here, frills or no frills attached. Naturally the seafood items are top drawer. The resort even has its own lobster grotto, where the lobsters await the call to dinner. That's about as fresh as you can get it. And all Four Seasons offer alternative cuisine, for sodium-, cholesterol- and calorie-conscious diners.

The endless array of activities at Four Seasons Resort Nevis includes the appropriate water sports such as snorkeling, windsurfing, boating and waterskiing; a large free-form pool; tennis on 10 all-weather or clay courts, with the facilities operated by Peter Burwash International; and a complimentary children's activities program called "Kids for All Seasons."

But enough about the resort. Let's talk about getting there. If you live in New York, for example, you may take a direct flight on American Airlines or other carriers to San Juan, then transfer to an American Eagle flight to St. Kitts. If you're traveling from the Southeast, say, you'll probably need to fly to American's hub in Raleigh/Durham, transfer to a flight to San Juan, transfer again to St. Kitts. Once you arrive in St. Kitts you're met by Four Seasons staff and driven to the Waterfront Lounge, where you transfer to one of the 65-foot luxury motor launches direct to the resort's private dock. Now, three planes and a boat in the same day can be a lot like work. I wasn't surprised that many of my fellow guests at the resort were planning to stay for a week or two, or longer. The trick is to keep your layover time to a minimum, and the people at Four Seasons Resort Nevis will be happy to advise you. Your best bet is to do exactly what Christopher Columbus did: Call your travel agent. Just be sure to tell him that you're *not* going to Cathay. ■

Places To Play

The Caribbean

Antigua

Cedar Valley Golf Club
Cedar Valley, Antigua,
West Indies
(809) 462-0161
TYPE OF FACILITY: Semi-private
NO. OF HOLES: 18
DESIGN: Traditional
YARDAGE: 5,544-6,142
PAR: 70
PEAK RATES: $20 for 18. Cart $25. Club rental $10.

Martinique

Empress Josephine Golf Club
Point du Boit, 97229 Trois Ilets,
Martinique, French West Indies
011-596-68-3281
TYPE OF FACILITY: Public
NO. OF HOLES: 18
DESIGN: Traditional
YARDAGE: 5,225-6,640
PAR: 71
PEAK RATES: Greenfee $40. Cart $44.
ARCHITECT: Robert Trent Jones

U.S. Virgin Islands

Carambola Golf Club
72 Estate River, Kings Hill, St.
Croix, U.S. Virgin Islands 00851
(809) 778-5638
TYPE OF FACILITY: Semi-private resort
NO. OF HOLES: 18
DESIGN: Traditional
YARDAGE: 5,424-6,843
PAR: 72 (women, 73)
PEAK RATES: Greenfee $50. Cart $12.50 per person.

Mahogany Run Golf Club
P.O. Box 7517, St. Thomas, U.S.
Virgin Islands 00801
(809) 775-7050
TYPE OF FACILITY: Public
NO. OF HOLES: 18
DESIGN: Traditional
YARDAGE: 4,873-6,023
PAR: 70
PEAK RATES: Greenfee of $75 includes 1/2 cart.

Cruise Ship Golf

Some of the best golf resorts in the Caribbean (and some of the Caribbean's best golf) are portable

IF YOU'VE NEVER BEEN TO THE Caribbean before, there isn't a better way to experience it for the first time than from the deck of a cruise ship, the floating all-inclusive resorts that wander from island to island (and golf course to golf course) in search of *your* perfect vacation.

The advantages of a cruise are obvious: First, one price covers everything, from airfare and hotel accommodations—if you arrive a day or two early or depart a day or two late—to the seven to 10 meals served on board each day. You know exactly what you're going to spend (almost) before you leave home.

Second, cruise ships make port in the most famous and the most visitor-friendly harbors in the region, from Ocho Rios in Jamaica to St. Thomas in the U.S. Virgin Islands to St. Maarten to San Juan. If it is your first visit you'll see the best the area has to offer—albeit in encapsulated form—which goes a long way toward helping you plan your next Caribbean vacation.

Third, and most important for club swingers, is the opportunity to play a different island course every day, five days in a row (on a seven-night cruise).

A personal favorite among the available sports cruises is Norwegian Cruise Line's Tee-Up Golf Cruise, an eight-day extravaganza on the *M.S. Starward* that originates in San Juan and includes stopovers in some of the most recognizable ports on the map.

While the *Starward* is not one of the largest or newest ships in the Norwegian fleet, it is beautifully appointed, impeccably maintained and offers near perfect golfing destinations on its itinerary.

The pool deck is the jumping off point for many ship-board activities, although lounging is by far the most popular. Really, can't you just see yourself in this picture? What are you waiting for?

Embarkation begins in San Juan on Sunday, and a 10 p.m. departure and full throttle gets you to Bridgetown, Barbados at dawn on Tuesday. In Barbados you'll play at the Sandy Lane Hotel & Golf Club, and the golf groups are usually small enough (from four to 12) to warrant personal attention from the club pro (a different one each cruise) traveling along. You'll tee off early every day, leaving afternoons and evenings for other on-shore or on-board activities.

Wednesday is spent in Martinique at the Empress Josephine course designed by Robert Trent Jones, Thursday at Mullet Bay in St. Maarten (a Joe Lee design), Friday at Cedar Valley Country Club in Antigua and Saturday at the renowned George Fazio-designed Mahogany Run Golf Club in St. Thomas.

Evenings are filled with variety and comedy shows in the Cabaret Theater, dancing until dawn in one of the clubs and lounges, gambling in the on-board casino, bingo, first-run movies, electronic horseracing, seminars or any combination of the above.

Dining can be elegant in the main dining room, Windows on the Sea (breakfast and dinner), or casual on the pool deck, and the midnight buffet, especially your last night at sea, is one of the highlights of the entire cruise.

It may seem initially that seven nights at sea is too long; by night two you'll find yourself wishing for at least another week's worth. Don't worry. If you don't get enough your first time out, you can always go back. You deserve it. ■